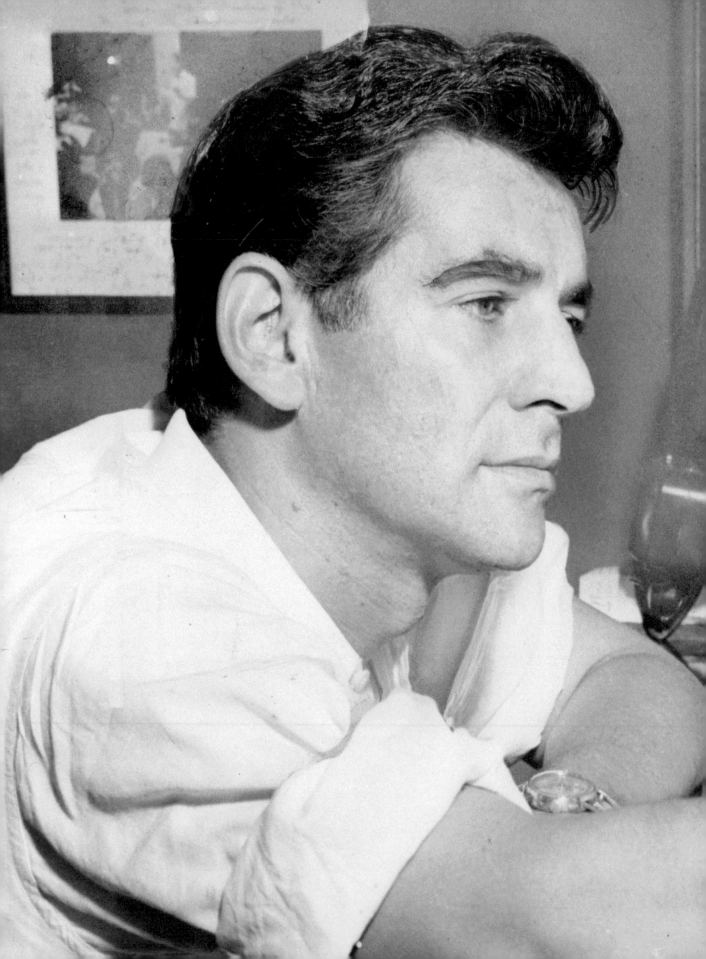

"I'm no longer quite sure what the question is, but I do know that the answer is Yes."

Leonard Bernstein

WAIT.

While standing on one foot, we ask, impatiently, "what's this about?"

We don't go to a movie unless the coming attraction tells us exactly what to expect.

We don't listen to music we're not sure we'll like.

And we want to know how to pigeonhole every idea and every book so we can move on and click.

Please, wait.

Let it simmer. It might not be for you, but at least this time, postpone the relief of resolution.

This is your opportunity to make something that matters.

ALSO BY SETH GODIN

Permission Marketing

Unleashing the Ideavirus

Survival is Not Enough

Purple Cow

Free Prize Inside

The Big Red Fez

Meatball Sundae

Small is the New Big

All Marketers are Liars

Tribes

The Dip

Linchpin

Poke the Box

We Are All Weird

V is for Vulnerable

The Icarus Deception

Watcha Gonna Do With That Duck

WHAT TO DO WHEN IT'S YOUR TURN

(AND IT'S ALWAYS YOUR TURN)

BY SETH GODIN

THE DOMINO PROJECT

WWW.YOURTURN.LINK

#yourturn

Ship.
Speak up.
Stand out.
Build a following.
Market a product.
Make a connection.
Solve an interesting problem.
Write, sing, invent, create, ask a
question, launch a project, organize a protest,
open the door for someone, question authority,
make a short film, direct, produce, create, or adopt.
Learn a new skill.
Help someone who needs you.

Be missed if you're gone.

YOUR TURN TO MAKE A RUCKUS.

It's easy, it's fun, and it's guaranteed to work. Of course you can do it.

All of that is true except for the part about easy, fun and guaranteed.

This is a book about an opportunity. The opportunity to take your turn and to make a difference. The opportunity to contribute, to lead and to live your life fully.

The thing is, there's no easy way to do this. No simple way to quiet the noise in your head, no proven method to earn the respect and applause of your family and friends, no guaranteed approach that's going to insulate you from heartache.

This might not work.

It might not be fun.

I hope you'll do it anyway.

BRO

ESCA

THE

KEN
ATOR
ORY

TWO PEOPLE ARE ON A ESCALATOR. We know that they are executives because in addition to being well dressed, they each appear to be stressed and in a hurry.

Suddenly, with a lurch, the escalator comes to a stop. Both executives are now trapped on a broken escalator, apparently unable to get to safety. The first executive sighs in frustration, while the second starts calling for help. Here are important people, executives, unable to get to where they need to go because the escalator has broken and there is no one to fix it or rescue them.

In 2006, Tim Piper turned this modern parable into a commercial for a company called Becel. The virality of the video is a testament to the absurd truth of Piper's vision. Too many of us are unable to see that all we have to do is walk right off the escalator. The stairs are there, they're part of it. They're not as automatic or as convenient as a functioning escalator, but they beat being stuck.

This is a book about seeing the stuck, getting unstuck, and working within and swimming upstream in a system that often would prefer that you merely stand still. It's about realizing that it's your turn, always your turn, and understanding that once you see the opportunity, it's yours.

Most of all, it's about freedom and our almost automatic insistence on avoiding it at all costs.

The opportunity is freedom

The freedom to connect, to reach out to just about anyone in the world.

The freedom to create, to sing and write and invent and share widely.

The freedom to lead, to stand up and say, "follow me."

The freedom to learn, to take almost any course on any topic and to put that learning to work.

The freedom to choose your next project, the information you consume, and the people you associate with.

We live in a world that's still filled with barriers and limits, a culture where too often people are judged, stripped of their dignity, and denied true freedoms. But at the same time, the economic and technological shifts around us have created an entirely new class of ruckus makers and have given people the freedom to stand up and acknowledge that it's their turn.

Now, more than ever, more of us have the freedom to care,

> the freedom to connect,

> the freedom to choose,

> the freedom to initiate,

> the freedom to do what matters.

If we choose.

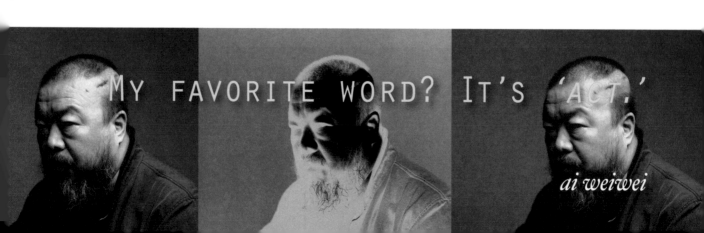

MY FAVORITE WORD? IT'S 'ACT.'

ai weiwei

The problem is freedom

Not that we don't have enough freedom but that we can't handle the freedom we have. Or more accurately, we *believe* we can't handle it.

Freedom brings the appearance of risk,

freedom brings responsibility,

freedom means we must make a choice.

FREEDOM IS OUR PROBLEM AND FREEDOM IS OUR OPPORTUNITY.

Liberate yourself from the need to be right.

Freedom and change

Usually when we say "it's your turn," we mean that it's your turn to be picked, to be the next one, the person who fits in more than any other. The next pop star on the cover of *Seventeen*, the next news anchor, the next plant manager. Or the next customer at the deli. This is the model in which you wait for change to happen to you.

Another model of "your turn," though, is the model of the person who **makes** change. We seek the change that is interesting, the change for the better, and most of all, the change that connects us to someone else. This is the freedom to make change, and the willingness to seek out the tension it brings.

TENSION AND TENSION AND TENSION CREATES CHANGE. CHANGE CREATES TENSION AND

Man's brain lives in the 20th century; the heart of most men lives still in the Stone Age. The majority of men have not yet acquired the maturity to be independent, to be rational, to be objective. They need myths and idols to endure the fact that man is all by himself, that there is no authority which gives meaning to life except man himself. ... modern man still is anxious and tempted to surrender his freedom to dictators of all kinds, or to lose it by transforming himself into a small cog in the machine, well fed, and well clothed, yet not a free man but an automaton.

Erich Fromm

The fear of stupidity

Stupid is not uncommon. Stupid is the way we feel when working on a difficult problem. Stupid is the emotion associated with learning—we are stupid and then we are not. The pre-learning state is stupidity.

A scientist might work ten years on solving a problem of math or logic or biology. Or a lifetime. And until the problem is solved, she's stupid. And then she isn't.

Which is all fine, actually.

The problem comes with the emotion that we're supposed to feel when we feel stupid: Fear.

We are supposed to be afraid of stupid, to get stupid over with as soon as we can.

Change, of course, makes everyone feel stupid, because change breaks all the old rules, inventing new ones, rules we don't know (yet).

And so the equation is obvious: Change —> Stupid —> Afraid.

One way to avoid this is to avoid change.

One way to avoid this is to avoid freedom.

The best way to avoid this is to embrace stupid and skip the last part.

There's nothing to be afraid of. Nothing except avoiding the feeling of stupid. And stupid is a good thing.

Andrew, Casper, Calvin, Jeni, Andy, McKenzie, Reggie
Red, Allison, Yi, Quinn, Matt, Leanne, Chelsea, The Ambassador

Taking your turn

It's rarely given to you.

Allison is like every other Ph.D. student, except she's also building a multi-state non-profit that is, store by store, extinguishing smoking and saving lives.

Calvin lives in Silicon Valley, but his new app is the opposite of a selfish move to get to an IPO. Instead, he's using technology to make it easier to do what he's always done... find friends that matter and let them know you care.

Reggie is an artist who refuses to wait for an art gallery to pick him. His work is followed by tens of thousands of people, and he's traveling the world, sharing it with them.

Red is just like Reggie, except her work is on video, is seen by millions and she's got advertisers calling her up demanding to work with her.

Jeni went to law school the same way a thousand thousand other people went to law school. But she took her turn to build a grassroots organization that fights global warming door to door, in communities.

McKenzie and Quinn don't look like the people who are changing the way schooling is done in the UK, but rather than patiently wait to be picked, they've decided to do it anyway. Thousands of teachers have already been trained by their company.

Andy shipped his newest project, a subscription service for gourmet meal ingredients. Lots of people have a plan to do something like this, but Andy actually did it.

> THE COST OF BEING WRONG
> IS LESS THAN THE COST
> OF DOING NOTHING.

Chelsea cares about beauty, and has built an organization that creates it daily. Sugar Paper has grown from a one-woman letterpress shop into a high-end provider of paper goods for celebrities and for people who admire beauty.

Casper is at the Harvard Divinity School, but unlike his classmates, he's not only asking the hard questions, he's building a spiritual movement to tackle them. Before he's ready.

Andrew sees a way for non-profits to spread their ideas using books. And one organization, one page at a time, he's turning that idea into action.

Matt invented the no-meat athlete movement and then took it to a higher level, spreading the word and building a tribe.

Leanne cares enough about animals that she's building a world-renowned fashion brand around the idea. And every season, she grows it in new directions.

Yi realizes that millions of people are dying because of poor sanitation. So, one country at a time, her team is working to eliminate it, forever.

The ambassador sees a different way for people in corporations to bring their humanity to work, and he shares that vision, with relentless generosity.

And what is the difference between these folks and you?

The t-shirts, for one. The willingness to take their turn. The knowledge that it might not work. And the delight (yes, I said delight) in dancing with their fear.

No, these people, in fact, all the people you admire, aren't better than you. They're merely willing to live with the duality of work/not work, they care enough to fail, and they're focused enough to ship their work and take their turn.

Making everything okay

There are three problems with freedom:

THINGS OFTEN DON'T TURN OUT PRECISELY THE WAY WE HOPE.

RESOLUTION TAKES TOO LONG.

AND WE MIGHT FAIL.

And so, when it's our turn, we take a pass. It's far more reliable to stay where we are than it is to leap, to jump to a new place different from the one we're in.

But there's an alternative. The alternative is to assume yes [and] no. To bet on failure [and] not failure. To realize that there's a third state, the state of not knowing, of not landing, of not yet.

Not everything has to be okay.

Perhaps it might be better for everything to be moving.

Moving forward, with generosity. Moving forward, with a willingness to live with the tension. Moving forward, learning as you go.

The person who fails the most, wins.

How big a roller coaster?

I hope we can agree that a roller coaster that fails to thrill isn't much of a ride.

But who decides what thrilling is? Why do some people crave ever bigger coasters while others have trouble with even a small one? I confess that I went from being hooked on them, the bigger the better, to avoiding them altogether as I got older.

The element that makes them thrilling, then, isn't the coaster; it's the experience we create in our head.

And that experience comes from encountering two things at once: the knowledge that this thing is tested, safe, and proven, combined with the innate feeling that at any moment, we're going to die.

Together at the same time.

Fun, not fun.

Work, not work.

Successful, not successful.

Without this tension, there's no true freedom, nothing happening when it's our turn.

FEAR

Concrete dreams

The safest dreams we experience are dreams with no hope of coming true. The dreams of superpowers, of omnipotence, of immortality. The teenager who dreams of stardom but never puts in the work isn't dreaming, he's hiding.

Superman is a safe bet, because none of us will ever have to become the Man of Steel or fly off a building.

Concrete dreams, on the other hand, are based on effort and a keen sense of what is possible. *Concrete dreams juxtapose the what if with the maybe*, they expose us to hope and to risk at the very same time.

Living with the possible takes guts.

Yes, it's personal

Can we just say that out loud?

When it's your turn, it's *your* turn. You own it. Your choice. Your freedom. Your responsibility.

We're taught to question ourselves. Worse, others are taught to question us. Those that traditionally haven't been in power are reminded of this daily. A study by linguist Kieran Snyder found that in written performance reviews, women find their personal style criticized *thirty times more often* than men do. Women discover that the criticism gets personal, regardless of the gender of the reviewer.

Whenever the status quo is threatened by an outsider, the insiders fight back. If you are doing things right—if you are upsetting the status quo—you will be criticized for your hoodie or your lack of education, your accent or imperfect background. They call names, denigrate, and put up barriers. Of course, it shouldn't matter what you look like, what matters is that you're taking your turn.

The Houston police arrested Ella Fitzgerald in her dressing room (for playing dice, but mostly to humiliate her). Pundits didn't take Shirley Chisolm seriously in her run for President. People who don't act like those in power, look like those in power or talk like those in power are treated as a threat.

Until the new normal arrives. It's not fair, it's not right, but it's true.

Change hurts. Do it anyway. It's personal and it matters.

You've been hacked.

People in power have taken advantage of glitches in our personalities and errors in our instincts to create an environment where they profit and we come out behind.

Politicians count on our short attention span. Banks know that we're impulsive. Bosses exert power over us based on our fear of failing. They all fuel a culture that keeps us in hock.

"THE AMERICAN PEOPLE ARE SUCKERS"

Hack back.

Many powerful organizations fear a truth-teller. They work hard to avoid being confronted by an individual who sees the world as it is and by a person who cares enough to change things.

Most of all, they have no plan for dealing with someone motivated enough to walk up the broken escalator.

Go.

The cost of a broken promise

You've almost certainly heard of the marshmallow test, research done by Walter Mischel over more than forty years at Stanford University. The short version: Small kids (three to five years old) are put in a library and offered a deal: Here's a marshmallow. If you eat it now, we're done, but if you wait fifteen minutes and the marshmallow is still here when we come back to you, you get two marshmallows.

It turns out that this single indicator of self-control and the ability to resist resolution is incredibly accurate. Twenty years later, the kids who showed they could wait ended up being happier, wealthier, on a better path forward.

New research (bit.ly/sethmarshmallow) makes something very clear, though: Kids who didn't think the promise of two-for-one would be kept ate the marshmallow right away. Of course they would, wouldn't you?

The home you grow up in and the culture you live in matters more than we can imagine. If you are raised in a chaotic environment filled with broken promises, it's incredibly difficult to bet on the future.

Industrialists made all of us promises as we grew up. Promises about the rewards of doing well in school or being obedient. Promises about good jobs waiting for us, about upward mobility, about fairness.

As the industrial era fades, those promises are being broken for too many.

The opportunity that the connection economy brings with it offers a different sent of promises, promises about freedom and taking your turn and doing work that matters. And it's not at all surprising that so many are hesitant to take action... we eat the marshmallow instead because, hey,. we're used to our system breaking its promises.

Of course we're wary of a glistening new offer, especially when in involves so much fear and requires us to trust others (and ourselves).

YOU

SCREWED UP, KID

YOU TRUSTED US

A bird in search of a cage

So much freedom, so much choice, so many opportunities to matter.

And yet, our cultural instinct is to find a place to hold us, a spot where we are safe from the obligation and the opportunity to choose. Because if we choose, then we are responsible, aren't we?

The cage keeps us in, certainly, but it also keeps everything else out. It protects us from a world that we've decided offers pitfalls, not opportunities.

Kafka wrote about the cage in search of a bird, a trap that was incomplete until it had found something to trap. But the reverse is more true, and sadder still. We're often birds that are unhappy until we find a cage that takes away our freedom.

Intention

It's possible to take your turn on purpose. To not wait for Harry Belafonte to cajole you. To bring focus and intentionality to your life and to become the kind of person who matters.

The doctor doesn't accidentally do surgery on you. The first violinist doesn't practice only when she's in the mood. The pilot doesn't work to make the flight safe only when a supervisor is watching.

It's possible to change your posture and your approach and your expectations and to choose to take your turn, to show up on a regular basis, and to make magic daily.

We talk about taking your turn, not being given your turn.

Four steps

Monika Hardy puts it this way: Notice, dream, connect, do.

We fail to *notice* because we're busy keeping busy.

We fail to *dream* because dreaming implies that we have to take a risk to realize our dream.

We fail to *connect* because we might get rejected.

And we fail to *do* because we haven't noticed, we haven't dreamed, and we haven't connected.

Finding your passion

Is it hiding?

It might be. Here's what someone wrote on my friend Michelle's Facebook wall: "I think you're passionate about your work and I know it turns people like me off."

Now we have two reasons not to find our passion. It might make us leap (and fail), and it might "turn people like me off."

In search of tension

Sooner or later, it comes to this: Great work is the result of seeking out tension, not avoiding it. Great work doesn't require reassurance, in fact, it avoids it

"I'm looking for something that might not work."

Worth it.

WHAT

OF P

DO YO

KIND
ENCIL
U USE?

The person who fails the most, wins

Stephen King, one of the most beloved, famous and bestselling authors ever, often goes to writer's conferences. After he talks for a little bit he says, "Any questions?"

Inevitably, someone raises their hand—I'm paraphrasing here—and says, "Mr. King, you are one of the most beloved, famous, and bestselling authors ever. What kind of pencil do you use to write your books?" It's almost as if knowing what kind of pencil Stephen King uses will help them be more like Stephen King.

People often go up to folks who invent and create and say, "Where do you get all your good ideas?" This is a really bad question.

The right question is, "Where do you get all your *bad* ideas?" Because if you have enough bad ideas, you'll have absolutely no trouble having enough good ideas. That's what people who create do, they let the ideas out. They sit and they do the work and the ideas come.

Bad ideas, good ideas, it is not yours to judge until later. Right now, your job is to only produce. After you produce, you can curate. You can select. You can censor. But now, have bad ideas. Lots and lots of bad ideas.

The second half of that rule: once you've got the best that you have you must ship it, interact with the market and engage and see what happens.

The rule is simple: the person who fails the most will win. If I fail more than you do, I will win. Because in order to keep failing, you've got to be good enough to keep playing. So, if you fail cataclysmically and never play again, you only fail once. But if you are always there shipping, putting your work into the world, creating and starting things, you will learn endless things. You will learn to see more accurately, you will learn the difference between a good idea and a bad idea and, most of all, you will keep producing.

No such thing as writer's block

Some people need to be motivated. Or so they think. They need the right cosmic alignment and the proper mood to do their creative work.

Actually, some people tell themselves this, but it's a form of hiding.

Motivation, Zig Ziglar used to say, is a lot like showering. It's useful, but it doesn't last, so you need to repeat it often.

If you find that motivational books and talks and a circle of people help you get going, by all means, use those tools; they worked for me and they might work for you. But they're not necessary.

There are two things that are necessary:

A. to see the cultural and economic shift and to realize that it is, in fact, your turn;

and

B. to develop a habit. A habit of showing up on a regular basis, of writing when it's time to write, raising your hand when asked, pitching in every single time. The habit is part of what it means to do work. Your posture of leaning into this opportunity, of connecting and creating and picking yourself: this is your work. How motivated you are today has nothing to do with the opportunity and the obligation you face.

GROW
UP

Growing up

Embracing the fear of freedom, deciding to determine your own path, this is the work of a grownup, of someone who can identify what truly matters. Being a grownup has nothing to do with how old you are—it's a choice, one that some people never get around to making. The productive grownup stops waiting for help and contributes instead.

There's a huge difference between being childlike and being childish. When we embrace joy and look at the world with fresh eyes, we're being childlike. When we demand instant gratification and a guarantee that everything will be okay, we're only being childish.

The noise

Here's the noise inside your head speaking:

1. I need a guarantee that embracing freedom is going to work if I go ahead and take advantage of it.

2. I need to be in the mood.

The noise will get neither of the two things it demands. There is no one to make a guarantee, no one in charge, no one who can honestly say, "it'll all be fine."

In fact, if you need reassurance, you will certainly suffer.

Suffer, as in the Buddhist term "dukkha." When we seek to hold onto something that is changing, when we try to find our footing on ground that's not stable, the mismatch between what's happening and what we wish for can be painful.

Why do what you're told? Because it comes with the promise of stability, the promise of finding your footing and the safety that comes with it.

BUT
WHY
SUFFER

We may mistakenly believe that the alternative to freedom, the path of merely doing what we're told and constantly seeking stability, is a better way to spend our lives.

Of course, it's not. It's not because the people who are promised stability rarely receive it. The promises are broken, again and again, and we've learned not to believe them. The people who are told that everything will be okay are always disappointed when it's not.

We suffer because we expect something to happen, and it doesn't.

Sorry. Heads, you suffer; tails, you endure a journey filled with unpredictable outcomes. At least one path—the one in which you embrace freedom even when it doesn't always pay off in the short run— offers you the juiciness of being alive, of experiencing the unexperienced, and most of all, of giving the world something it cares about.

And what about getting in the mood? What about the motivation you'll need to engage in this life? *Our need for motivation is due to our need for reassurance.* We are paralyzed by our fear that it might not work, and we let the fear demotivate us, giving us the perfect excuse to not create.

"MOTIVATION IS FOR AMATEURS."

Chuck Close

Setting the mood when you're not in the mood

What a day you've had. Just about everything was a hassle, the weather is no good, and you think you're coming down with a cold. Your date stood you up for dinner and the cab sprayed you with water as it drove by without stopping.

You're completely entitled to the bad mood that's enveloping you.

On the way into your apartment, the phone rings. It's a good friend, someone you haven't heard from in a while. He's just calling to tell you what a great guy you are, how much you mean to him. He doesn't want anything other than to say hi.

And then you open the door to your apartment and you see that your roommate has invited six of your favorite people over for a surprise-for-no-reason dinner party. The room is filled with smiles and love and the smell of your favorite tagine.

How's your mood now?

Here's the real question: if all it takes to turn a lousy day into a great one is a little dinner party and a phone call, why would you ever choose to have a lousy day? Even better, why would you let someone else have a lousy one?

The people who need you need you to fix their mood, even when you don't feel like it. And we need you to learn to fix your own mood so you can be the one who fixes the rest of us. The mood-fixer is a precious resource, and you can learn how to be that resource.

Do what you should do. Your mood will follow.

WE WIN THE INFINITE GAME

"Guarantee that this will work."

It's the essence of every *Dummies* book, of every reassurance, of all the prodding we do before we even sign up to do the work.

Consider the famous-college paradox. Colleges publish their typical test scores and are ranked by how hard it is to get in. Those rankings change the very makeup of who applies, because high schoolers (like all of us) don't like being rejected. There's a huge gap between the many who are qualified and the few who apply. "I won't apply, I might not get in."

By all means, we need to conserve our resources and not create a series of impossible projects (which, by itself, is another form of hiding). But if the only cost of being rejected is the experience of being rejected, it's a foolish compromise to err on the side of doing only the things that are guaranteed to work.

Getting in the right mood to do creative work

Here's what doesn't work: Getting in the mood. Being adequately supported. Finding peers who will challenge you and push you and reward you as you explore new ways to take your turn.

The mythology of the brilliant, gifted creator of magic is a myth.

It's not about standing in the right light or being in the right moment to let the muse arrive. It's not about figuring out how to be comfortable enough to do the work.

In fact, we're capable of creating work that matters only if we're willing to be uncomfortable while we do it.

WHEN WE KEEP PLAYING

Beaten by a sock puppet

Well, I wasn't physically beaten about the head and face, but it felt that way.

Remember Lamb Chop, the incredibly annoying puppet that was a fixture on TV in the 1960s? (I hope you don't, just for your peace of mind, but either way, bear with me.)

In 1986, I was nominated for an American Film Institute award. This isn't quite the Oscars, but in the home video business, it was a big deal, with tuxedos and everything. The category was Best Home Video for Kids, and we were sort of a shoe-in, competing against a banal video featuring Shari Lewis and her sock puppet, Lamb Chop.

I flew out for the ceremony in L.A. Bruce Jenner and Gary Coleman (!) were the hosts, and they finally got to my category. They called out the nominees, and, as you've guessed from my foreshadowing, the winner was... Lamb Chop.

I was crushed.

The thing is, if I hadn't been nominated, I wouldn't even have noticed. If you had walked up to me on the street and said, "Lamb Chop won the AFI award," I would have said, "Good for the sock!" and walked on by, no problem.

The suffering comes from the mismatch, from the difference between the serene and certain and happy future that we expect, that we're counting on, that we're already half living in, and the reality of what happens when we take our turn.

Yes, you can walk up the escalator, but no, it's not always going to turn out the way you wish.

Sankhara-dukkha, the suffering that your fear causes

I wish we had an English word for this. How do you feel when things don't go the way you expected? When you use "should" and "shouldn't" to describe the way things are?

"It's my party and I'll cry if I want to" is a perfect song lyric. It captures the juxtaposition of high expectations and a reality that simply doesn't match our dreams.

If you sign up to take your turn, to walk up the escalator, to take responsibility for the changes you cause, then, yes, indeed, it won't turn out just the way you hoped. You won't get picked when you need it most, and promises of perfection will turn out to be false.

The thing is, this suffering is all invented. It's all based on expectations you set in advance, not on what actually happened.

Invented suffering?

Of course, not all suffering is invented. The suffering of humanity and families and injustice can't be minimized or overlooked. I'm only talking about the suffering we induce in ourselves, the suffering we create because of how we perceive freedom.

The first form of this suffering is the anxiety of experiencing failure in advance. The tortured twisting and self-recrimination, judging ourselves for things we haven't even done yet.

When we talk about suffering for our art, this is a huge part of it. The narrative of failure, of shame, of not-our-turn. The cultural baggage that we all carry about humility and hubris, about speaking up, and being seen as a fraud.

A second form of invented suffering is the pain of feeling owed. Of having leapt, taken our turn, done our very best work and not getting the results we expect (and deserve).

The first narrative, the danger and fear and oppressive anxiety often push us away from contributing. But when we do contribute, having experienced so much in our internal narrative, our instinct is to demand gratitude.

And prizes.

And an end to the suffering we've created.

When success doesn't occur, the easiest thing is to walk away and not make the mistake of speaking up ever again. The most important thing to do, though, is to do it again, to care again and to seek to make change, again.

Marcel Duchamp and the delay

Many call Duchamp the most important artist of the twentieth century. He certainly made us think.

One of his most notorious forms of work was called a "readymade." He'd put a urinal or a household item into an art exhibit and call it art. He wanted us to comment and to examine what it meant to make or engage with a work of art.

Recently, I learned that he also created a group of pieces he referred to as a "delay." There are lots of theories about what he meant by this, but I'm pretty sure he was talking about dukkha and resolution.

When you see a pretty picture, you understand immediately what the painter was saying. When I tell you a knock-knock joke, the time in between "who's there?" and the punchline can be measured in seconds.

There's no tension, no real disconnect between what you came to expect and what was delivered.

In work that really matters, though, the disconnect grows. There's a delay, a delay in between the time we're aware of a rift in the universe and the moment that rift is resolved and we can say that everything is okay.

That delay, the hallway, the moment of indecision, the time when we get it and don't get it at the same time, that's what freedom feels like.

Samuel Beckett is still waiting

When will Godot come?

Does waiting for him increase the likelihood that he'll show up? Does it increase his obligation to show up?

Or is the waiting the entire point?

Like the delay, like the hallway, Godot is worth it because he might never come. It's the might of it that makes it worth the journey to sit through the play. The end isn't the point, of course. It's the journey, the tension, the *mightness*.

Voted down

Justin Cheng and his fellow researchers at Stanford found that when social media sites enable downvoting, their worst users get even worse, because they feel like martyrs.

They deal with the tension of a no vote by getting worse, because it's easier than believing that they can actually get better.

In search of a quick resolution (or no resolution)

Resolution relieves tension, and we've been taught that tension is a bad thing.

And so, we want to know, and soon, how we're doing. We want the novel to end and the hero to win and the next story to show up on our news feed. We want, most of all, for the silence to end.

The silence used to be precious, it used to be at the heart of our joy and our humanity. The silence of a father and a son, walking down the beach, side by side. The silence of sitting and wondering. The silence of 'what happens next?'

It's been replaced by the cheap thrill of 'what happens now?'

Instead of basking in the tension, waiting for the reviews to come in or the feedback to happen, we push forward, insisting that we get it quicker. A newspaper is too slow, the TV news is too slow, we need to monitor Twitter to see it first.

To end the tension.

But Godot works and Duchamp works and most everything wonderful works because the tension is part of it.

How much is it worth to you to release the tension, right now? What happens to your work if you're able to wait a little longer?

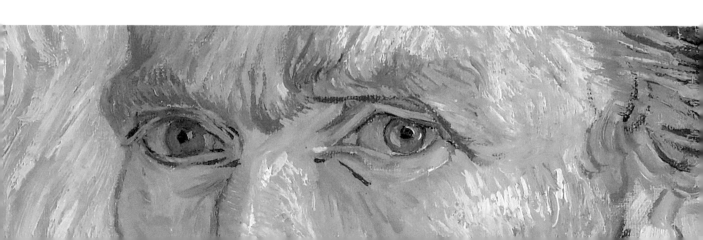

Unprepared

Is there anything worse we can say about you and your work?

But the word means two things, not just one. There is the unprepared of a final exam, of forgetting your lines, of showing up to a gunfight with a knife—this is the unprepared of the industrial world, the unprepared of being an industrial cog in an industrial system, but a cog that is out-of-whack, disconnected, and poorly maintained.

What about the other kind, though?

We are unprepared to do something for the first time, always.

We are unprepared to create a new kind of beauty, to connect with another human in a way that we've never connected before.

We are unprepared for our first bestseller or for a massive failure unlike any we've ever seen before. We are unprepared to fall in love and to be loved.

We are unprepared for the reaction when we surprise and delight someone, and we are always unprepared for the next breakthrough.

We've been so terrified into believing in the importance of preparation that it's spilled over into that other realm, the realm of life where we have no choice but to be unprepared.

If you demand that everything that happens be something you are adequately prepared for, we wonder if you've chosen never to leap in ways that we need you to leap.

THE BOOK THAT WILL MOST CHANGE YOUR LIFE IS THE BOOK YOU WRITE.

If we don't dare to try, it's our own fault

The problem with the ability to take your turn is simple: it makes things your fault. Not just the things you do, but the things you don't do.

Politicians learned a long time ago that the best way to get elected is to make everything someone else's fault. Blame it on those people, or the culture, or the government. Anyone but me, please.

And yet, this new economy that showed up uninvited keeps reminding us of something frightening: if you want to sing, sing.

There's no doubt that cultural and societal impediments give some people (like me, for instance) a huge advantage. Where you grew up, who your parents were, how people judge you... all of these things are real, not imagined.

That doesn't change the calculus of what's changed, though. What's changed is that more people than ever have a device that connects them to the town square. They have access to information, to courses, to opportunities that weren't even imagined just twenty years ago. Twenty years!

It's an extraordinary thing to waste. And we're mostly wasting it. Wasting it by waiting for a guarantee.

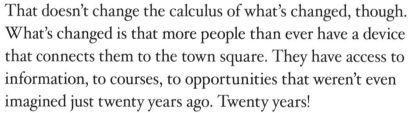

"DESTINY IS IN OUR OWN HANDS.
IF WE DON'T SUCCEED*,
IT'S OUR OWN FAULT."

Elon Musk

*Careful about how you define success! It should be *your* definition of a thing worth doing, not someone else's. Invent it, don't accept it.

Are you taking it seriously or are you taking it personally?

By all means, the leap is serious. But when it doesn't work, it's nothing personal. It might feel personal, that's what our lizard brain wants, but is it really? Must it be?

Watch a kid play a board game and you see what happens when serious and personal intersect. It's not that the game is being lost, it's that *he* is losing. The outcome of the game is a personal one, a referendum on his worth as a human being.

When the work is this personal, doing it well becomes difficult. That's because our fear of the outcome leads us to hide, to, ironically, depersonalize our work, because it's all too much to bear.

When we merely take it seriously, though, approaching the opportunity the way a professional does, we can bring our full intent to the project at hand.

If we can live with failure, we're actually more likely to avoid it.

Pythagoras and the fifth hammer

Pythagoras, the guy who invented the hypotenuse, led a cult of brilliant but sometimes confused mathematicians. They believed that harmonics held the key to understanding how things functioned. At the heart of their work was the study of ratios, of dividing things into their basic components in search of the harmony of the universe.

According to the myth, Pythagoras was stuck on a theory, and he went for a walk to clear his head. He passed a blacksmith's shop and heard five workers inside, all using hammers to bend iron. As their hammers struck in unison, the clang organized into a beautiful sound, with all the hammers singing out in harmony at once.

He walked into the blacksmith's shop and, with a bluster that would have been fun to watch, took all five hammers away with him.

He wanted to study what made their harmony so

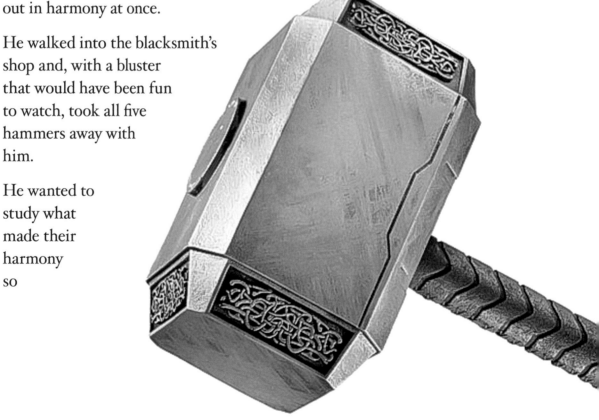

beautiful... it might unlock the secret he was seeking.

Over the following weeks, Pythagoras weighed and measured each hammer. He wanted to understand why they didn't sound identical and, more important, why they sounded so good when they all clanged in unison.

His work helped us discover a physical connection between math and the world. It turns out that the ratios in the weights of the first four hammers led to their ringing in harmony—each had a weight that was a multiple of the other. More fascinating to me, though, was that *the fifth hammer didn't follow any of the rules*. The fifth hammer was spurious, data that didn't fit, something to be ignored.

Like many researchers throughout time, he threw out the fifth hammer (and the pesky mismatch) and published his work only about the first four. But it turns out that the misfit, the fifth hammer was the secret to the entire sound. It worked precisely *because* it wasn't perfect, precisely because it added grit and resonance to a system that would have been flaccid without it.

The harmonies of Crosby, Stills, Nash, and Young worked best because of Neil Young. Because his voice wasn't quite right. Because he's a loose cannon. His sound is not quite right, so it works.

During their breakthrough tour in 1974, the core trio traveled together, often by private jet, from gig to gig. Young refused to fly with them, instead leaving immediately after each concert and driving with his son to the next gig in an old mobile home. He was their friction, the wild card, the fifth hammer.

The fifth hammer is the one that's not proven, obvious or beyond discussion.

The fifth hammer is you, when you take your turn.

THE
FIFTH HAMMER
DOESN'T
CONTRIBUTE
BEAUTY AND
MAGIC BY
FITTING IN.
THE FIFTH HAMMER
MAKES A
DIFFERENCE
BY STANDING OUT.

Try this with $5

It might teach you something about what "no" means.

Go to the bus station and walk up to the first person you meet. Say to him, with as much confidence and trustiworthiness you can muster, "would you like to buy this five-dollar bill? I'm selling it for a dollar."

The odds are, he will walk away without buying anything. In fact, he will probably avoid eye contact and walk away rather quickly.

How rude!

Doesn't he know that you're offering him a five-dollar bill for just a dollar?

Of course people won't buy a five-dollar bill from a stranger at the bus station. It's the first rule of the bus station: don't buy something that feels like a scam. The second rule is don't talk to strangers.

That story got there before you did.

Do you understand that the 'no' that you heard wasn't someone rejecting you, or even rejecting your new project after carefully and completely reviewing it?

It was the 'no' of someone examining your story (as heard) and comparing it to their worldview.

You never had a chance.

Consider this alternative...

Go to your neighbor's house with a $5 bill in a plain, unsigned envelope. Leave it in his mailbox.

Go back again tomorrow.

Do it one more time the day after that.

Then, on the fourth day, ring his doorbell, hand him another $5 and say, "I'm the guy who keeps leaving you five-dollar bills." Smile and walk away.

On the fifth day, ring his bell and say, "Hey, wanna buy a $5 bill for a dollar?"

My guess is that it'll go a lot better than it did at the train station.

The five-dollar bill later in this story is worth just as much as it was at the beginning. What's different is the *story*, not just the story you're telling, but the story he's hearing. It's weird (you're weird) but it feels a lot safer this time, doesn't it?

Everything you create, every idea you try to share, every project you launch is a five-dollar bill. Sometimes, people will refuse it, even as a gift. Other times, they'll fall all over themselves to pay you ten dollars.

They buy (or reject) a story. Not you.

THERE IS NO TERROR IN
THE BANG, ONLY IN THE
ANTICIPATION OF IT.

ALFRED HITCHCOCK

Fear of failure

In the industrialized world, the world of driveways, parkways, dishwashers, and dumbwaiters, a rational fear for our individual survival isn't even in the top ten. Wild animals don't threaten our existence, the diseases that were rampant a century ago do not exist, and crime in our biggest cities is more rare than ever before.

So what is there to be afraid of?

Failure.

Our schools, our marketers, and our culture reinforce this fear daily. The heartbreak of psoriasis, the humiliation of underarm odor, but most of all, the utter horror of trying and failing.

Failure is almost never as bad as we fear it will be, but it's our fear that we feel, not the failure.

Worst of all, we've so amplified our internal narrative that we can't help but associate freedom with failure.

And so our fear of failure transfers effortlessly into fear of freedom.

Consider our avoidance of feeling tired. If you're unwilling to be tired, unwilling to feel fatigue in your legs, you can't run a marathon. Successful marathon runners haven't figured out how to avoid being tired, they've figured out where to put the tired when it arrives. If you're not willing to be tired, you can't run.

If you're not willing to imagine failure, you're unable to be free.

In just a few generations, we've gone from "The only thing we have to fear is fear itself" to "The fear we feel is the fear of freedom."

What happened at Solvay?

In 1927, the Solvay Congress in Brussels assembled 29 physicists. This photo captures the all-star line-up, titans including Heisenberg*, Einstein, Curie and Bohr.

Seventeen people in this photo won the Nobel Prize in Physics.

*There is some uncertainty as to whether Heisenberg was actually there.

The extraordinary thing: Many of these people won the Nobel Prize after the conference was held.

They didn't get invited because they had won the Nobel Prize. They won the Nobel Prize because they got invited.

PEOPLE LIKE US DO THINGS LIKE THIS.

The hard part

Every time I invite people to apply to a seminar or offer an internship , I'm surprised to discover that many of the applicants have no hard skills to brag about. They're happy to check off boxes like, "business development," and "making a ruckus," but they rarely say that they know how to code, or to use CSS or even InDesign. They've spent so many years following instructions, fitting in and getting good grades that they failed to learn to do anything that independent.

The side effect of a lack of hard skills is that these very same people almost never have much to show for themselves in the way of a project portfolio, online or off. They can't point to something and say, "I made that."

More people make a living from non-manual labor today than ever before. Sometimes, though, we forget that the only way to successfully move forward is to do emotional labor, to put in the effort and emotion to make something that matters and something that might not work. Today, we have the chance to do work that's far more pleasant and involves far more freedom. And the only one stopping us from doing this work—is us.

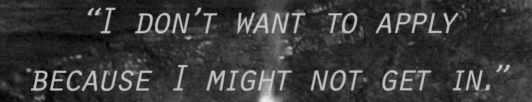

"I DON'T WANT TO APPLY BECAUSE I MIGHT NOT GET IN."

Exchanging our pain

The pain of not reaching our potential, the pain of being overlooked, the pain of not being heard.

The pain of being a cog, of not fitting in enough, never enough. The pain of having to measure up in a world that keeps telling us that we don't.

So many live with that pain because the alternative is hard to consider.

The alternative is to experience the pain of being free. The pain of saying, "here, I made this." The pain of living with the opportunity to make a difference.

There's no pain-free path. But at least you can do something that matters.

Yertle

In New York, it's the top of the real estate market that keeps booming. Specifically, penthouses, the very top floor, with the high ceilings and great views.

I watched as a building was going up the other day, and wasn't surprised to see that the top floor was significantly taller than the floors below. Penthouses have bigger windows, too.

Here's the thing: When you're in the penthouse, enjoying the windows and the view and the high ceilings, you have no idea whether there's an apartment above yours. In fact, it probably shouldn't matter, should it?

But it does.

Like Yertle the Turtle, who not only needed to be high up but also needed to be on top of everyone, the penthouse dweller is paying for supremacy, for being the unqualified winner on top.

> The need to be recognized as the winner destroys your ability to take your turn, because taking your turn requires you to be willing to not win.

> My argument is the only long-term way to make it as an artist is to do it from a position of generosity, of seeking to connect and change people for the better. But generosity, while it sometimes leads to it-feels-like-winning can never be based on winning, because winning requires other people to lose.

> Yertle-style.

Fear is the mind-killer.

Fear is the little-death that brings total obliteration. I will face my fear.

I will permit it to pass over me and through me.

And when it has gone past I will turn the inner eye to see its path. Where the fear has gone there will be nothing.

Only I will remain.

Frank Herbert

THIS:

Avoid certainty.
Pick yourself.
Postpone gratification.
Seek joy.
Embrace generosity.
Dance with fear.
Be paranoid about mediocrity.
See the world as it is.
Be the boss of you.

OR THIS:

Seek certainty whenever possible, mostly by giving others the power to pick you, relieve tension, and give you instructions.

When it's available, take gratification. Order dessert tonight, diet tomorrow. Honk your horn, argue with your ex, slam the table, and find a reason to teach people a lesson because it feels good and you're entitled.

Generosity is fine when it's aimed at you, but there always seems to be a reason to focus on something you need more than taking the time or investing the effort to help someone else.

And most of all, let fear (and the fear of fear) drive your decisions. Stand on the escalator, hollering, waiting for the man to come and set you free.

Not even close

In *Open: An Autobiography,* Andre Agassi wrote about the secret he learned while playing tennis: "But I don't feel that Wimbledon changed me. I feel, in fact, as if I've been let in on a dirty little secret: winning changes nothing. Now that I've won a slam, I know something that very few people on earth are permitted to know. A win doesn't feel as good as a loss feels bad, and the good feeling doesn't last as long as the bad. Not even close."

Ouch. It's so easy to believe that five great Amazon reviews don't compare in impact to one bad one. Five closed sales don't compare to one "no." What a sad way to choose to live life.

No wonder we don't want to speak up or stand up or do anything much that matters. We've persuaded ourselves that good feelings aren't even close to outweighing bad ones.

45 of 52 people found the following review helpful

☆☆☆☆☆ **Not Worth Reading,** July 15, 2010

By **jrlowry** - See all my reviews

This review is from: **Linchpin: Are You Indispensable? (Hardcove**

I've never written a review on Amazon before but feel c after throwing in the towel on this book 80 pages into it that so many reviewers enjoyed this book so much. I fe being shouted at throughout those 80 pages and told th again and again and again. To me, the book felt like litt series of sound bites anchored around a theme but not well at all. The examples, which I usually love in a book explained well enough for me to fully get the point if I v familiar with the person.

"I had no choice"

This, of course, is a wonderful thing to be able to say if your hope is to be off the hook.

When we talk about how we had no choice, how our options were constrained, how we were following instructions, or orders, or the map, it's not our fault. *It's not our fault.*

How delicious is that feeling? No freedom, no responsibility. You had no choice, so how could you possibly be responsible?

This stands in contrast to the plaintive admission, "I had a choice." When we have a choice, when we have the freedom to choose, we claim the responsibility that goes with it.

You've already guessed: we always have a choice.

It might be accurate to say, "if I wanted to keep x, y, and z, then I had no choice." Or, perhaps, "if I wanted to not rock the boat, not make a ruckus, not risk something dear to me, I had no choice."

But no choice at all?

We willfully create the illusion that we have no choice because it's frightening to be free. But the deeper we look, the more we realize just how much choice we actually have. The choice of which roads to take and, more profoundly, which ones we choose not to take.

The blog we don't start, the job we don't quit, the injustice we overlook. The course we don't take, the tutor we don't hire, the question we don't ask.

Every escalator goes faster if we also walk up the stairs on our own. And sooner or later, every escalator stalls. It's up to us to choose what to do about that, as the freedom is ours, always.

When is the right time?

The other day, I was speaking to two dozen interns at a famous investment bank. These kids were at the top of the heap. Famous colleges, involved parents, the right network. Here they were at a huge conference table, perhaps 25 feet long, in their blue suits and white shirts, the very center of the privileged universe.

By just about every measure, these twenty-year-old students have more options than most. Career options, family options, geography options—choice is everywhere.

I spent about half an hour talking to them about broken escalators and their freedom, about how they could choose to do their very best work, to become more than a cog in a (profitable) machine.

Hannah raised her hand. "But maybe it makes sense to wait. After all, we have student loans to pay off. It doesn't make sense to take risks now; later, when we're better established, *then* we can find our own path."

Here's the thing: It's never the right time. When you are starting a family, it's not the right time. When your kids are about to go to college, it's not the right time. When there's an elderly parent depending on you...

We have a thousand perfect reasons to give up our freedom in exchange for the illusion of safety. All of them are based on a misunderstanding of fear vs. freedom.

This is the chance of a lifetime, our lifetime.

Not someone else, us.

Not later.

Now.

Furious is not the same as fierce

Furious is your ego talking. It is the fight to get even, to reclaim the higher ground, to set things right.

Furious might look good on TV, but it rarely succeeds, because someone who is furious is unable to create art, to be generous, to see what's actually happening. All he wants to do is defeat his enemy.

My friend Asim spent a year in Pakistan. While there, he wrote one of the most classic lines I've read in our modern era, "I did a random search on the internet for boxing clubs." It turns out he found one in Lahore. Ehtisham, his host at the gym, an MMA fighter from Hunza, told him, "...gasping for breath and recklessly pacing back and forth, is counterproductive, you might as well throw in the towel."

No, fury doesn't work, but fierceness does.

The artist who is fierce is able to sacrifice his ego and his perception of safety to go to a place that frightens him. He cares so much about the work and the community and the opportunity to make a difference that he's able to be rational when everyone else winds themselves into a knot being furious.

Fierceness takes honesty and commitment. Fierceness means telling yourself the truth about what's at stake and what's possible, without expending a drop of energy on trying to make everything okay.

Because everything will never be okay.

And everything is always okay.

Fierce means living with the simultaneous certainty that this is vitally important and this might not work.

It's always too soon

More than four hundred years ago, Gutenberg launched the printing press. What a foolish time to bring a book manufacturing system to Europe—96 percent of the population was illiterate.

When only one in twenty-five people knows how to use the product you're about to launch, and when learning how to use it (to read) takes years, it's clearly ridiculous to even consider this project.

When Karl Benz introduced the car to Germany, it was against the law to drive a car. He had to get a letter from the King granting him permission to use his new device.

And, worth mentioning, no one knew how to drive a car. And there were no roads. And no gas stations.

Again, a foolish time to launch that project, no?

There is a fundamental difference between being ready and being prepared.

You are more prepared than you realize. You probably aren't ready, and you can't be ready, not if you're doing something worthwhile.

Because we always do our best work and take our turn before we're ready.

Backstage with Dylan

How many times do you have to perform in front of 15,000 people before you're relaxed in the hours before you go onstage? No pre-show jitters at the 3,000th show, certainly.

It's not the show that makes us nervous. It's our story about the show, and doing the work makes that story go away.

Bravery and courage are for other people

It's entirely possible that you are physically able to be a thoroughbred's jockey or lead a battalion into battle or work the night shift as a cop. These are risky and difficult jobs, and they require bravery.

And it's more than likely that there are tasks you're avoiding doing because they require significant emotional labor and the ability to overcome perceived risk. They're not physically dangerous, but they require courage nonetheless.

It's easy to use words like "bravery" and "courage" because they pigeonhole the work. It is work for the brave and for the courageous, not for us.

By labeling yourself as not-quite-brave or almost-but-not-yet couragous, you let yourself off the hook. It's a label, and it's a label for other people, people who are in a better place than you are, apparently.

Getting off the broken escalator requires neither bravery nor courage. It's not risky. It merely *appears* to be risky.

I'm not asking you to be a brave person or a courageous person. I'm not pushing you to be some sort of creative genius when you believe you're actually not.

No, the opportunity lies in merely seeing what's actually happening. False perceptions leading to a cycle of fear that's baseless.

You don't need a permit or a blessing or any sort of permission to decide to take your turn. You only have to open your eyes and look. And then choose.

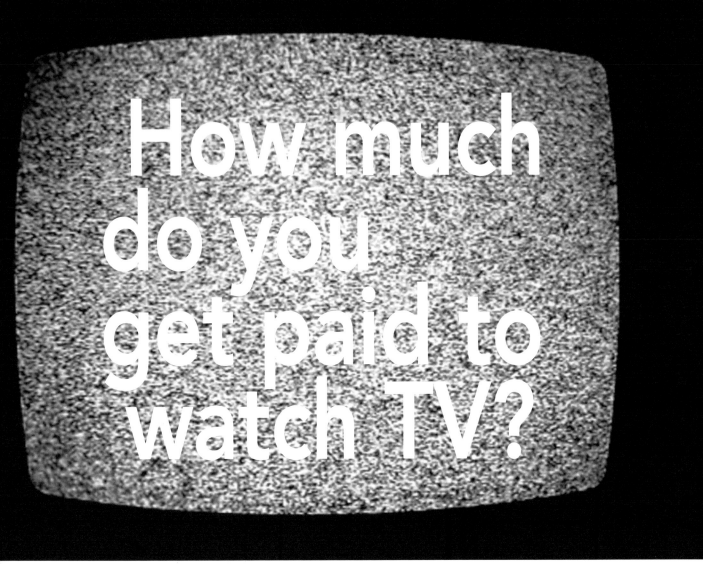

How much do you get paid to watch TV?

What does **better** mean?

It used to mean, "meets spec." It used to mean, "more reliable." It used to mean that you had successfully complied, created something scarce and could profit from it.

Today, better means more connected. Something we would miss if it were gone. In the connection economy, better means more human, more vulnerable, the thing that embraces the tension of works/might not work.

We can always do better.

Sometimes people ask why they should create or contribute if they're not going to get paid for it. They hesitate to write a novel if no publisher will pay them for it, and they sneer at the mere amateur who does what he does for love, not for money.

We've commercialized all the things that used to be passions. You're supposed to get paid to be a sculptor or a golfer, a writer or an impresario, the creator of projects.

And if we're getting paid for these intellectual pursuits, then we're taught we ought to treat them the way workers in the industrialized world have been trained to treat their jobs—with disdain, with an awareness that we ought to do less for more. What a shame, what a foolish way to dishonor our humanity.

Instead, just for a moment, imagine what would happen if we decided to and create and connect merely because we love it. It turns out that acting as if we love it creates the environment where that might actually happen.

What does the market say?

It's pretty easy to focus on the story that the market tells us about our work. The story of criticism or rejection or even success.

More important, I think, is the story we tell ourselves. A story of mattering, of resilience, of daring to take a turn.

Sure, the external story matters, mostly because it has an impact on the story we tell ourselves. But your narrative belongs to you, and it's up to you to create and live a story that works .

Write until you are not afraid to write

Perhaps you will always be afraid. How about this: Write until you are able to write words you are proud enough to share.

Don't hesitate. Don't decide the words aren't good enough yet. Write.

Then write more.

After that, after you've written and written, then you get to decide. And if it's not good enough to share, write again.

Isaac Asimov got up every morning at dawn and wrote until noon. Every day. He published 400 books in his lifetime, by showing up on a regular basis. His best work surprised him, every time.

Do what you should do

Morita therapy was developed in Japan in the 1920s. The essence of the approach is that productive people are able to distinguish between their feelings and their need to do their work, to show up with mindful effort.

At night, clouds can float in front of the moon, but it doesn't change the fact that the moon is still there. There's nothing at all we can do about the clouds, and trying to will away our anxiety or to wait until we're in the mood to do our best is an invitation to frustration.

Shomo Morita taught his patients that our emotions, like the weather, have nothing to do with our need to do the work, to live our lives. Emotions like fear and anxiety come and go, and we can note them, but we don't need to battle them or obsess over them, particularly when they become an impediment to creation.

If fear is able to keep up us from showing up when it's our turn, then fear has won the day and it will return again and again. Morita took a different approach: When fear arrives, do what you should do. Note the fear, welcome it if you can, but do what you should do.

It's noisy out here

Which means you've got to figure out how to make it quiet in there.

There are two places to find our footing, to get the stability we seek.

The most common way: We can buy into the industrial system, seeking to comply and find safety in the promises made by others. We can work to make everything okay by finding and grabbing a sinecure, a niche where the world will leave us alone.

How's that working out for you?

The alternative is understanding that the world isn't going to provide this haven. The only reliable way to find our footing is to create it, to change the story we tell ourselves, to build an internal foundation that not only tolerates a crazy world filled with change, but embraces it.

The sailor doesn't mind a rough sea. It's not because he's physically different from you—it's because the rocking of the boat is expected. We naturally find our own horizon when the external one is rocking.

Suffering comes from the impossible juxtaposition of a world that can't possibly live up to our unreasonable expectations.

"THE EXPLORER IS THE PERSON WHO IS LOST."
Tim Cahill

AVERT YOUR EYES

What will you create?

Who will you help?

What connection will you make?

What will you dare to care about?

There are so many opportunities, so many chances to find beauty or to ease suffering, that the easiest thing to do is to pretend that they don't exist.

Because if they *do* exist, if that little girl will live a better life because you showed up, if that void will be filled because you cared enough to do something about it... if we actually recognize the opportunity that's in front of us, what are we to do about it?

We'd have no choice but to change things for the better, to take our turn and make a difference.

You have the chance to change things

As Michael Shrage has pointed out, that's what all great organizations do. Artists and humans too. We make change.

What do you care enough to fix, or disrupt, or invent?

Starting right here, right now. If we are willing to suffer enough to matter, we are able to make change happen. Or at least we can try.

Don't avert your eyes. Look at the opportunity. Take it.

It's yours.

On living in two futures at once

Every time you take your turn, you're seeking to make a change happen, and there's no guarantee that it will.

Which means, there is a fork in the road:

THIS MIGHT WORK.

THIS MIGHT NOT WORK.

And beyond the fear of failure is the tension of living in two different futures. In order to engage with our ideas, to flesh out our approach, we start envisioning how it will work, what it'll feel like. We begin to live inside that future.

A future that might not happen.

"It will all be okay"

This oft-repeated phrase might mean, "everything will turn out the way you want it to." But it doesn't. In fact, it *never* turns out that way.

It actually means, "something will happen." And whatever happens, you can figure out what to do with that. Because by defining what happens as "okay," we open the door to accepting our work and our world and our quest to make things that matter.

IF YOU CARE ENOUGH TO RISK FAILURE,
CHOOSE TO DO EXCEPTIONAL WORK.

I SEE IT ALL PERFECTLY; THERE ARE TWO POSSIBLE SITUATIONS— ONE CAN EITHER DO **THIS** OR **THAT**. MY HONEST OPINION AND MY FRIENDLY ADVICE IS THIS: *DO IT OR DO NOT DO IT—YOU WILL REGRET BOTH.* … TO DARE IS TO LOSE ONE'S FOOTING MOMENTARILY. NOT TO DARE IS TO LOSE ONESELF."

SØREN KIERKEGAARD

IF YOU CARE ENOUGH TO DO EXCEPTIONAL WORK, CHOOSE TO RISK FAILURE.

It's all invented
(but that doesn't mean it isn't real)

A friend grew up with a severe phobia. He told me that one of the most hurtful things adults said to him (they meant well, no doubt) was, "it's all in your head."

Just because it's in your head doesn't mean you're not sick, in pain, unable to breathe.

The paralyzing fear we feel in the face of freedom is in our head; that's the only place it could be. It's something we invented, just as we invent all of the drama in our lives, all of the attractions, connections, and meaning that we depend on.

Ben and Roz Zander talk about the game we play in creating a narrative of our lives. We invent our expectations, our rules, our standards. We invent what we hope will happen, what needs to happen, what has to happen.

Most of all, we invent the constraints that prevent us from seeking freedom. We *invent* them.

If these inventions aren't working, if they're making us sick or unhappy or ineffective, the question on the table is: why not invent something else?

Why not invent different rules, different expectations, different ways of deciding what success is and what it's not?

Here's how I know that there's no correct set of inventions: We each have a different list. Each of us has different expectations, a different definition of fairness, and a different set of goals. And my set (and probably your set) is not the same as it was a month or a year or a decade ago. It changes.

If each of us has a unique, invented worldview, and that worldview keeps changing, why not change it on purpose? Why not invent a way of being that's actually eager (not just comfortable, but eager) to live with the duality of work/not work, to embrace the freedom of living in a world where we're not controlling every outcome and not even sure about what's going to happen next?

Creative, dynamic, and happy people have invented a monologue built around taking the work seriously, not personally, and in accepting that it will all be okay. Because, after all, what's the alternative?

That story that keeps replaying

Your story, that story that keeps replaying, the interaction of your expectations and what happens, the narrative, the disappointments and the way you process it...

It's all invented.

Ambien, the popular sleep aid, doesn't actually help people sleep much more (in one study, it boosted sleep by 18 minutes a night). No, the reason it works is that it's an amnesiac.

Ambien makes you forget that you didn't get a good night's sleep.

Because a huge side effect of sleeplessness is the invented story we tell ourselves about how tired we are. Ambien doesn't help us sleep, it just destroys the negative story about not sleeping.

It's all invented. It's still real, the pain is real, the frustration is real, but the story that's causing it all is something we made up, and something we can change. The pain is real, and so is a path to changing it.

Free will and the play-by-play in your head

Back to freedom and what it means.

Everyone I've ever asked has had the same experience with the voice in their head. They tell me that the little man (or woman) who's up there, constantly chattering, makes the important decisions. "I feel like having some ice cream," he says, and so we have some ice cream. It's this voiceover that considers options, debates outcomes, and ultimately decides. Or at least it feels that way.

But Dan Dennett and other philosophers and researchers have demonstrated that this isn't true.

Here's how to think about it: Dave Hodge (substitute your favorite sportscaster) is doing the play-by-play for a baseball game. Now, take a video recording of the game and move Dave's play-by-play forward by about six seconds. Instead of Dave describing what happens *after* the play (the way it usually works), in our sped-up version, Dave says something and then it happens.

"Suzuki is on the mound, winds up for the pitch, it's a strike..." we hear Hodge say. And then, we watch Suzuki wind up and throw a pitch.

This, of course, is silly. We all know that the announcer doesn't tell the player what to do; we know that the player does something and then the announcer describes it.

Guess what? That's how the voice works. It does play-by-play.

That voice in your head is describing what you're about to do after a different part of your brain has already initiated that action.

And that's how we drive ourselves nuts, and why we hide, and why it's hard to be free. Because the chattering voice in our head is busy pretending it has agency, when in fact, all it's doing is going along for the ride.

Take a second to digest that, because it will change everything. Your body decides, the voice in your brain narrates.

Of course, there's a cycle. The voice in your head then pushes back on the rest of your body, often causing stress, or second-guessing, or hesitation. It's only when we learn not to banish the voice but to dance with it that we're able to do our best work.

When was the last time you did something for the first time?

When it's your turn, the cultural instinct is to to launch the safe balloon, to keep your head down and create a predictable response. To play a greatest hit, not something new and dangerous.

And that's a shame.

It's your turn to write a blog post, call an old friend, start a podcast. It's your turn to say thank you, to apologize, to ask a difficult question. It's your turn to help a competitor, to find value where it's been overlooked, to teach someone who is waiting to be taught.

There are countless reasons not to do this. Practical, time-based, financially prudent reasons to avoid just about all the things you're avoiding.

But the opportunity is profound.

It's the opportunity to dance with your fear, to look people in the eye and to do work that matters.

John Bingham is the father of the Slow Running movement. He doesn't win races, but he enters them. He doesn't train through the pain or seek to diminish those who might be slower than he is. He has embraced the freedom (at middle age) to become an athlete.

His motto is that he had the courage to start.

John got it slightly wrong. It's not that he had the courage to start, because no courage is required to run around the block. No, the miracle is that he started.

'Courage' ought to be reserved for overcoming real risk, for doing something dangerous. Making a choice about the story we tell ourselves doesn't take courage. It merely requires we see what's going on and make a choice.

> "THE MIRACLE ISN'T THAT I FINISHED. THE MIRACLE IS THAT I HAD THE COURAGE TO START."

He began, one foot, the other foot, started.

He was aware enough to see that he, like just about every healthy person his age, was capable of running around the block, and his anticipation of running, even a block, had transformed into anxiety and into fear and into "I have no choice, I'm stuck here." John ended that cycle.

John's transformation was from believing that he wasn't the sort of person who could run a block into realizing that there are only choices, not predestined sorts of people. It's merely a choice.

It's all a choice.

OBLIGATION IS A PRIVILEGE AND A CURSE

Who owes you?

My friend Rohan Rajiv posted this on his blog:

> A lot of human unhappiness is caused by thoughts of what the world and the people in it owe us. These thoughts are caused by the world view – "I am a good person. I've done good for … and, so, … owes me for it."
>
> This world view causes expectation and this expectation results in inevitable disappointment. It is also foolhardy for many reasons; the first of which is that we vastly over estimate the effects of our actions.
>
> Things get much better when we internalize 2 truths –
>
> 1. Nobody owes you anything (no, not even a thank you)
>
> 2. It is actually you who owes the world and its denizens. You take up space (physical and emotional). And you better have something good to show for it.

Something about Rohan's post really resonated with me, but there's a lot wrapped up in the four words, "Nobody owes you anything" and I want to try to deconstruct this statement.

Obligation is not a two-way street

We do good work when we repay a debt.

But the feeling of being owed destroys our ability to do good work. It's not a paradox; it's an opportunity to redefine what we mean by good work and how we feel about being owed a debt.

If you're doing your work, taking your turn, with the expectation that someone else is going to appreciate you, change your life, or otherwise respond, you're setting yourself up for failure. Because sooner or later (probably sooner), you will be let down, and then what?

If you do what you do because you want other people to do something, you're stuck. Because you can't control other people, and giving them the power to decide if you will continue to produce good work is foolish.

No, nobody owes you anything when it comes to your art.

It turns out, though, that you owe all of us quite a bit.

THE FEELING OF BEING OWED IS TOXIC

The toxicity of feeling owed when the debt isn't repaid

Obligation drives much of what we do. If we owe something to someone, many of us want to repay that debt.

Incurring obligation is something most of us feel quite viscerally. We feel like people owe us something because of our effort or our skill or a favor we've done.

And so we ask ourselves: Do we owe this teacher respect? Do we owe our spouse loyalty? Do we owe our nation patriotism?

At the same time, we keep track of who owes us and what we're owed.

How do we process the feeling of being owed? When we've leapt, taken a risk, done something generous for someone else, what does she owe us in return?

Inevitably, not all of our debts will be repaid. Eventually, people will let us down; they will interpret their promises or their obligations differently than we do. *And the feeling of being owed is toxic.*

Four kinds of obligation

The problem with this analysis, though, is that there are many settings in which people actually do owe us, sometimes quite a lot.

Consider four kinds of obligations each of us encounters every day:

Social (or cultural) obligation

Legal obligation

Moral obligation

Artistic obligation

Social obligation: If you walk into the library, you're expected to whisper. Of course, it's not against the law to talk loudly, but you'll be shushed. You owe it to everyone else in the library to be quiet. You bought into that social contract the moment you walked into the library.

All day long we try to interpret and live up to our social obligations. We say "thank you" to strangers, we smile at babies, we hold the door open for someone arriving just behind us. We do these things even if we don't feel completely motivated, and we do them without believing that there's a significant upside awaiting us in return.

Legal obligation: Sign a contract with someone, and yes, she does owe you something. Open a store, and yes, the people who take something from the shop do owe you a payment in return.

Legal obligations are cut and dried enough that we don't have to sweat them very often. Society cares enough about these obligations that it has written them down and created consequences for those who don't obey.

Moral obligation: This is just a social obligation with generations of time on its side. The obligation to not kill a puppy, to take care of our family, to look out for people who can't look out for themselves. Can we agree that we have these obligations, to our community and to each other?

When people violate a moral obligation, we ostracize them, and rightly so.

Artistic obligation: This is the one that really matters to our discussion. We needed to break out the other sorts of obligations so we could get to the core of what's holding us back, which is an expectation of what others should do when they encounter art.

What do we owe the singer who trained for years to sing us that song? What do we owe the person who spoke up at the meeting with a brand new idea? We have all sorts of moral and cultural obligations, but the artist must act as if:

WE OWE HER NOTHING.

We might, in fact, want to applaud her, encourage her, motivate her to do it again. We might buy from her, endorse her, or cheer the artist on.

And if we do, that's great...

But the productive artist refuses to incur an artistic obligation. She acts as though the audience doesn't owe her anything, and forgiving them in advance gives her the freedom to make the work she needs to make.

The flipside, though, is also true. The productive artist must act as if she owes the audience, and in unlimited measure.

MAKE
BETTER
ART

If the audience doesn't respond, the artist ought to make more work anyway. You, the artist, ought to do it again. And again. Not because you're owed, but because you owe our culture (and yourself) the art.

As Neil Gaiman has said, when it doesn't work, make better art.

You don't take your turn because you're going to get an obligatory encouragement. No, you take your turn because you can. Because it's your obligation.

The nature of a gift

The best gift requires little of the recipient. The giver doesn't say, "I worked hard to bring you this gift; you must love it, use it, embrace it. You must be grateful to me in recompense for how much I put into this gift. This gift controls you."

Of course not. The best gift is accompanied by, "here, I made this. Do with it as you will."

When you overstate the obligation of the audience, of course they'll let you down, and when they do, you don't have to show up again. What a great excuse to stop making your art, to hide...

It's not your turn to win, or your turn to be picked, or even your turn to be guaranteed gratitude...

IT'S MERELY YOUR TURN TO GIVE A GIFT.

Far better than they deserve

The drugstore near my house has an antique tin ceiling. It has a long-time staff of caring, literate professionals. They stock the obscure and the wonderful.

And at the drop of hat, people walk away from all that to save ten cents on shaving cream at the local Walgreen's.

The artisan at the farmer's market has a little booth, but there's always a table with free samples, a chance to taste something new, engage with the farmer and buy something.

Every week, people descend on the samples, eat all they can and walk away, with no intent at all of ever buying anything.

An author works for years on a book and a callous critic attacks it, without even reading it.

The audience in the theater, distracted by their cellphones, talks through the entire movie, never giving it a chance.

The craftsman puts extra effort into the welt of the shoe, the shoe that will be worn by someone who will never, ever appreciate it.

And don't forget the boss who creates a magical workplace, not just stocked with snacks and a free lunch but with respect and opportunity—only to discover that employees, used to the old regime, take advantage of the freedom to do less, not to create and invent.

But sometimes, somehow, against all this bad behavior, we persist. We persist in creating things that are generous, wonderful and out of the box. We make things better than they need to be. Not because we expect to be repaid, or because the market deserves it or is even part of the bargain. *No, only because we can.*

INVENTED OBLIGATION

Making promises that the market can't keep, won't keep or doesn't even know about

If you are expecting a response, counting on gratitude, seeking applause, you've just made a promise on behalf of someone who isn't actively part of the conversation, who didn't sign up for this deal. You've given power away to someone who doesn't care as much as you do.

In the traditional scarcity-based economy, the exchange is everything. "If you do this, I will do that." If you give me corn, I will give you money. If you sign up for this, I'll deliver it to you...

That's not going to go away. Mutual promises drive our culture.

But this transaction focus robs us of our ability to create true gifts, and worse, it gives us a place to hide. We can say, "they don't get it, they won't do it, they didn't come through." Most of all, we say, "they don't deserve it." And so we back off and start complying instead of creating.

"This casting agent has taken advantage of my goodwill in the past," "this customer will never be through town again, and he's a lousy tipper, I can tell." And so we push ourselves away from connection, we sell ourselves short because people always let us down.

What if we don't give them a chance to let us down?

Miles Davis sometimes performed with his back to the audience—he was letting them go, forgiving them, playing to play, not for applause.

"Here, I made this," can be the beginning and the end of the conversation. You got to make it. *That's* your compensation. You got to take your turn. You dared.

That's enough.

IS OUR CHANCE TO HIDE

ARE

YOU

THIRSTY

ENOUGH?

"One day, I'll be ready"

That's what she said to me.

After four years of college, a year of interning, and an arduous six-month job search, she finally had her job, as assistant to a talent agent. I asked her, "what's the big goal, what are you after?"

Her eyes lit up. Apparently, most people she ran into merely demanded a cup of coffee.

"My dream is to be an agent, to do what my boss does. I want to do what he does."

Well, why not start now? Why not find clients now? Develop small projects, and find ways to get them in front of people who might want to produce them? Why wait?

Because, apparently, you're supposed to wait.

You don't take tenth-grade math until you're in tenth grade. (Or at least wait until someone tells you to take advanced math, noteworthy merely because someone picked you to do it.) You don't do the job until you're offered the job. You don't lead until you're asked.

The thing is, as the only good line in *The Treasure of Sierra Madre* says, "Badges? We don't need no stinkin' badges...."

There's no permit required to be a talent agent. Or a leader. Or an impresario. There's no authority who announces that it's your turn to do much of anything.

For most people, it never happens. Sometimes, because they're confused and honestly believe that they have to wait for the call.

But mostly, it doesn't happen because they're not thirsty enough.

THE INTERNET
MEANS YOU CAN
LEARN ANYTHING
YOU WANT, IF
YOU ARE THIRSTY
ENOUGH TO DO
THE WORK TO
LEARN IT. WE
DON'T NEED
BADGES.

Lucy is thirsty

I went to Kenya to work with Western Seed, a startup backed by Acumen, a non-profit I work with. Western Seed sells seeds to hard-working farmers in the beautiful and fertile farm belt of Kenya. The seeds they sell produce two or three times as much corn as the 'farm-saved seed' that farmers have been using for thousands of years. Traditionally, seed in these communities is saved from year to year, while the company sells a natural hybrid seed similar to the kind that has been sold for fifty years in the US. Buy a bag of seeds and you can turn your farming from subsistence break-even to profitable. It's a life changer.

I went to a meeting of farmers, perhaps 25 in all, organized by Western. These were farmers using traditional methods, people who were in the heart of Western's target market. As I talked to them, I was surprised to discover that they had no idea what the other farmers, their neighbors, were planting or whether their strategies were working or not. This lack of knowledge would be unheard of in most farm communities in more industralized countries. Farmers there are scientists, obsessed with data, constantly thirsty for what's going to work better and sharing the data with each other.

The next day, I met Lucy. Lucy is now one of the wealthier people in her village. She owns a tree farm, a taxi, several cows and puts all nine of her kids through private school—on precisely the same amount of land as her neighbors. Lucy's not unique in her success... there are countless farmers just like her in Kenya, but she is a pioneer.

"It's simple," she told me. "I want to provide for my family, so when I can test something new, something that might improve my harvest, I test it."

Apparently, it doesn't matter much whether someone is a programmer in Manhattan or a farmer in Kenya. Thirst is optional, and thirst is the essential element of taking your turn and making a difference.

The secret of teaching (and the secret of learning)

I've taught all my life. I've taught canoeing, juggling, marketing, snaps, leadership, computer science, and even the spoons. I've taught kids and college students and older adults. And I've discovered that there's one thing (and only one thing) that separates successful students from the the unsuccessful ones.

The good ones show up and say, "teach me."

They look at failure and confusion as temporary conditions and say, "that didn't work, show me another way."

They are thirsty.

The other students have their arms crossed. They want to know if it's on the test. They are restless. They need to be sold before they can be taught.

And in fact, that's most of what happens in organized education. If you can't sell it, people don't learn it. When frustration (the twin sister of learning) shows up, most people stop trying.

Online education is supposed to change everything, right? More than 100,000 people regularly sign up for advanced computer science courses online, courses that are taught by great professors and are free to all who enroll. Shockingly, 99 percent—99 percent!—of the students drop out before they finish the course.

Not thirsty enough.

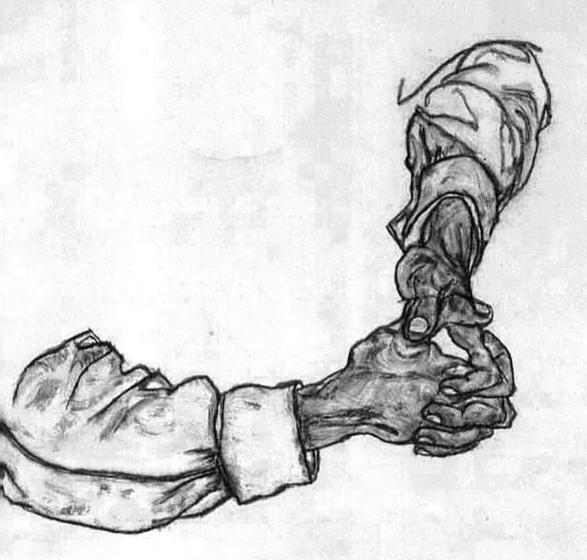

Tell the truth

We don't know what you see. We have no idea what you're thinking. We need your contribution, your vision, your truth.

Yes, for a long time, for most of your life, we demanded you ask for instructions and that you comply.

We're ready now, though. Ready for you to show up and to lead us. Ready for your contribution. We are ready for you to tell us your truth.

Not *the* truth, but *your* truth, the truth of the world as you see it and as you wish it to be.

No place to hide

Have you ever been that place where this no place to hide?

"I made this."

"It's my fault."

"It was my idea."

"I decided to do it."

How often do we bend over backwards to avoid uttering these words? How often are we unwilling to face the void, squirming under the gaze of an authority figure as we fight for our lives, hoping that we won't get blamed?

No place to hide is the only place to be.

If it matters, we have to remove every single cubbyhole, every nook and cranny where we can escape.

It's only when we are this naked that we're able to fully take our turn and to understand what it is to make something. If it's worth doing, it's worth doing this naked, this alone, this responsibly.

I know you don't want to do this. None of us do, at first. We've been trained to avoid this at all costs, I get that.

But now it's become a crutch and a drag on what you're capable of.

Go, get naked.

.64

.54 .55 .56 .57
.58

.39

.38

ARE YOU
WORKING TO
CONNECT THE
DOTS OR TO
MERELY COLLECT
MORE DOTS?

.45

.13

.14

.50 .48

.15

.51 .49 .47

.35

.33

.34

.53

Where does thirst come from?

It's almost impossible to go to a class and be taught to be thirsty for knowledge. It's almost impossible to read a book that ignites desire.

Thirst comes from culture. It comes from our parents and our peers. It comes, sometimes, from growing up in poverty, but often, more often, it comes from growing up without poverty. Ironically, having too much, having too many resources, can also slake our thirst and suck away our desire to learn and grow and contribute.

Thirst comes from habits. The habit of asking why. The habit of shipping. The habit of leading.

Everyone, regardless of background or culture, is capable of becoming thirsty. It's not based on gender or income or even a desire to win.

We are capable of being thirsty. In fact, it's an obligation.

Where does thirst go?

Fear is the thirst killer. Broken promises, too. False hopes, dashed.

We know how to extinguish thirst, and sometimes it seems like we go out of way to do so:

> Punish someone for asking why.
>
> Be afraid of where people you love might go if they grow.
>
> Focus on grades and outcomes, not processes.
>
> Correct grammar instead of rewarding inquiry.
>
> Consume instead of produce.
>
> Give blame instead of taking responsibility.

THE DEVIL DOESN'T NEED AN

Hot wash, intent and thirst

What's better—finding out that everything is okay (you got an A) or learning something?

It's quite a profound fork in the road. The prevailing system of the educational-industrial complex puts the fear of a 'C' in us. The entire point of twelve (or sixteen) years of our lives isn't to learn anything, it's to get an A.

Is it any wonder that thirst disappears?

What if instead, we decided to opt in to a different path, the path of always learning?

Hot wash is a process of continuous improvement that's often used by the armed forces. At the end of every exercise, all parties concerned engage in an ego-free discussion of what could go better.

This is quite difficult to do in a room filled with people who'd rather get an A. The requirement, then, is that the room be inhabited by people who'd rather learn instead.

Thirst.

If your intent is to make art, to get better, to connect—if the goal is to learn something and to cycle on your way to learning ever more—then hot wash is easy and obvious.

"I'm curious," is a completely different way to engage than, "Is everything okay?"

Because everything is rarely okay.

DVOCATE... HE'S FINE.

Instigating, initiating, and being thirteen and female

Have you noticed that in the *Wizard of Oz* movie (and the book, as well), just about every decision, every instigation and every act of courage, is made by Dorothy, a teenage girl? She's the one who decides, the one who keeps pushing, the one who dumps water on the witch.

Embracing the freedom of a teenage girl was a revolutionary act in a movie in 1939. Unfortunately, it's still rare in the media today.

We watch this movie and quickly come to believe that Dorothy is sui generis, one of a kind, a breed apart. Obviously, this perfect heroine isn't like us, our sisters or our daughters. She's an idealized, fictional character.

Except that the essence of Dorothy is within all of us, regardless of age and gender. Most of us don't deal with flying monkeys and talking tin men, but all of us are afraid; all of us buy into self-doubt and the culture of waiting to be picked. The difference is that Dorothy (or L. Frank Baum, actually) decides that the mission is more important than the noise in her head. At every turn, Dorothy stands up and makes a choice, despite her fear, or sometimes because of it.

[AND YES, OF COURSE, IT'S TRUE, DOROTHY, YOU'VE HAD THE SLIPPERS ON YOUR FEET ALL ALONG, HAVEN'T YOU?]

" You ought to be ashamed of yourself ! "

The illusion of safety
(and the mistake of fear)

Loons, those beautiful birds that live in northern lakes, mate for life. The thing is, a small lake can support only one family of loons. If they sense that another couple has moved in, the first ones will probably leave, looking for months for a new lake to call home.

Their haunting nighttime call is remembered by everyone who has heard it, and there are CDs of loon calls for sale. If you take a recording and play it loudly across the lake, the loons will instantly call back, staking out their territory. Keep playing it, though, and the loons on the lake will make a terrible mistake.

They'll come to the conclusion that the other loons are there to stay, and they'll leave.

False evidence turns into fear.

And the loons aren't the only creatures who fall into this trap.

It seems so much easier to stand on the escalator and ask for help. But of course, walking up those stairs is actually easier and safer than waiting; it merely feels risky. Standing still is the riskiest plan of all.

When confronted with freedom, we make up things to be afraid of, we invent threats, we seek out things that might go wrong, all so we can avoid the fear of failure, all so we can push ourselves away from the opportunities right in front of us.

> THE FISHERMEN KNOW THAT THE SEA IS DANGEROUS AND THE STORM TERRIBLE, BUT THEY HAVE NEVER FOUND THESE DANGERS SUFFICIENT REASON FOR REMAINING ASHORE.
>
> *Vincent Van Gogh*

Where do you put the tired?

Everyone who runs the marathon gets tired.

Yet there are no books called, "How to run without getting tired." That's because you can't.

And everyone who takes their turn gets scared.

So why is everyone always talking about how to do important work, give talks, make a ruckus without the fear? *Of course you're going to be afraid.*

The thing is, to finish the marathon all you need to do is find a place to put the tired. Not avoid it, merely put it somewhere.

And the same thing is true for the important work we need to do.

WHERE
DO YOU
PUT THE
FEAR?

Working the hallway

There is a moment in between the time it's good enough and the time you ship.

This is the hallway, as you walk from the dressing room to the stage.

This is the penultimate meeting, the check-in before you go for final approval.

In this moment, when we're in the hallway, we're desperate for resolution. Desperate for the reassurance that will come from a smile in the audience or a nod from our boss.

It's like we've left one trapeze and we're flying in the air for the other one. For solidity. For safety. All our focus is on nailing the landing, getting this midair thing over with.

Not so fast.

Fly.

This is the moment to plus it, to add a little extra, or to refine. The moment to push a little harder, to simplify, to create elegance. This is our chance, now that we've paid all these dues, to become a magician, the one who's brave enough to say, "one more thing."

It's so much easier to start closing down, protecting ourselves, to put a little distance between who we are and what we made.

There are so many places to hide, by the time we finish walking the hallway the work already isn't ours. We're safe.

I'm not proposing you stall or delay. The deadline doesn't change. All that changes is your connection to the work, your willingness to use this moment to put your full self into the most generous, vulnerable work you're capable of creating.

The universe does not seek revenge on those who choose

What happens when the plane is oversold? It doesn't happen nearly as often as it used to, because it so completely freaks out the anxious traveler.

There are 150 seats and 160 people eager to fly. The lucky 150 are settling in, finally onboard, bags stowed, seats about to be reclined. The harried gate agent comes on the microphone and announces that for anyone willing to take a flight two hours later, she's willing to pay for the ticket ($500) plus throw in another $300 in compensation.

The math is pretty compelling, no? That's $400 an hour. How many people on this flight make $400 an hour?

No one raises a hand. No one volunteers. Right now, they have certainty. Getting off the plane, on the other hand, is inviting retribution; it feels greedy. Why trade away certainty, certainty that's so incredibly difficult to find?

People who are open to uncertainty are the pathfinders for the rest of us. They are the ones who walk on the moon, who start important non-profits, who paint paintings worth falling in love with. We stare at them with admiration and shower them with opportunities and gratitude...

NOT BECAUSE THEY TAKE BIG RISKS, BUT BECAUSE THEY ARE WILLING TO LIVE WITH NOT KNOWING.

Needs (vs. being needed)

Our internal narrative is loud, and gets louder when we ignore it. We have needs. We have wants that become needs as soon as our previous needs are met. And we have wishes, which become wants soon enough.

As Abraham Joshua Heschel has pointed out, there is a minimum set of needs that must be met for any organism to survive, but it's not clear that there's a maximum. And marketing, the billions of dollars of ads and interruptions that drive our economy, works overtime to increase our maximum, to remind us of our wants (or to invent them).

What's the point of needing more than anyone else needs? Needing gives away our authority and freedom. Being needed, on the hand, is an opportunity to contribute and to make a difference.

For some, being needed feels like too much obligation, too much of a promise, too much to bear.

And yet, those who are needed are rarely stuck on the escalator.

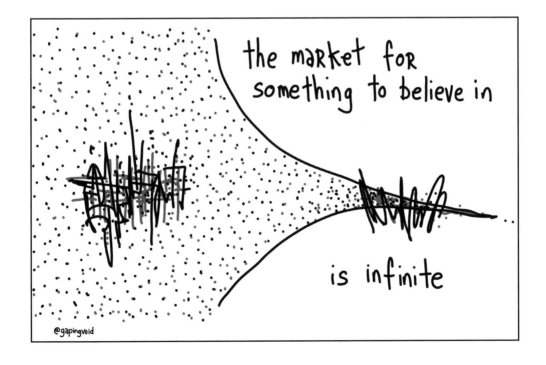

the market for something to believe in

is infinite

@gapingvoid

125

Saying yes

"We feel jailed in the confinement of personal needs. The more we indulge in satisfactions, the deeper is our feeling of oppressiveness. ... **we must be able to say no to ourselves in the name of a higher yes.**"

—*Abraham Joshua Heschel, Between God and Man*

The world around us regularly offers us opportunities to step up, to lead, to raise our hands. We get a chance to be needed and to do work that matters. And we rarely say "yes" to that opportunity. We hesitate because the yes offends our need to play it safe, our need to be picked, and, it's true, our need to work on our other, more urgent, needs.

If you are intent on resolving tension and dedicated to finding gratification sooner rather than later, it's extremely difficult to be in the mood for yes, to be open to the possibility of something you didn't plan for.

As we make our world smaller by saying no, it gets ever easier to be alone with our thoughts, to tend the garden of our fears and imagined inadequacies. No closes doors; no diminishes the external distractions that can take away from our internal chatter. No feels safe, but no is a way to amplify the noise in our head.

Yes is an invitation to the rest of the world. An invitation to be needed.

Luck school

Researcher Richard Wiseman writes, "My research revealed that lucky people generate good fortune via four basic principles. They are skilled at creating and noticing chance opportunities, make lucky decisions by listening to their intuition, create self-fulfilling prophesies via positive expectations, and adopt a resilient attitude that transforms bad luck into good."

In other words, you can learn to be lucky.

You can pay attention to opportunities to contribute, to moments where you can speak up and make a difference.

You can open yourself to the voice of intuition, largely by distinguishing it from the resistance, the voice of fear, the noise in your head that's prattling on to distract you.

You can create self-fulfilling prophecies by saying 'yes' and meaning it. Yes this might work, yes, let's try.

And finally, you can train yourself to be resilient so that bad luck is temporary instead of a fork in the road.

Go to luck school on purpose; do it with intention. You'll learn.

"WOULDN'T IT BE GREAT IF WE LIVED IN A WORLD WHERE INSECURITY AND DESPERATION MADE US MORE ATTRACTIVE?"

Broadcast News

The new normal

Normal is cultural; normal changes. We ask ourselves: Is this what people like us need? What people like us do?

In China, it's not unusual to see people spitting on the street. That rarely happens in Chicago or Miami. Is spitting a basic human function, or is it something we do because those around us do it?

No one had a smart phone (or UGGs or Nikes), and then "everyone" did. But of course, not everyone did. Most people on Earth still don't have one. But the "everyone" who surrounds that teenager or this executive has one, and it is now the new normal.

That's what cultural progress looks like. That's how we stamp out overt racism and how we build a business around yoga clothes: tribes, in sync, establishing a new set of expectations and a new set of needs.

And the fog of culture is so thick, yet so invisible that we don't even notice it's there.

That eleven-year-old girl is told, all day every day, that people like her need to be cute and quiet and compliant. That kid in the ghetto is taught what to expect from authority figures and is reminded every time he dreams bigger dreams. The privileged teenager in the suburbs grows up with an invisible set of standards and expectations about fitting in.

We created the stuck-escalator culture. It was built into our myths and our histories and our life lessons.

But the world is shifting and there's a new normal available if we have the vision to see what's possible, if we care enough to walk up the stairs instead.

As Gandhi said, "We need not wait to see what others do."

Given or chosen?

There's a huge difference between what you're given, born with, handed, part of the job, here for you versus what you choose to create, to build, to work toward.

I was working with a non-profit executive, and he said, "but our donors are people who believe x." And this was true at the time. It was in the rear view mirror, the world as it was.

If the organization is going to evolve and grow, it might very well need a different sort of donor, a donor who believes something else. And that's a choice, not something that will suddenly arrive of its own accord.

When we make a choice, we're far more likely to succeed if we announce that choice, if only to ourselves. Your choice, not ours, not dice.

I CHOOSE TO GO
IN THIS DIRECTION,

I CHOOSE TO SAY THIS,

I CHOOSE TO FIND THIS ANSWER.

Timid/reckless, tight/loose

Where does the artist live? How does Miles Davis or George Carlin or Madame Curie decide where to do the work?

Too timid and it's safe. Too reckless and it's also safe, because, of course, no one takes reckless seriously, do they?

Too tight and there's no room to dance, no chance to leap. And too loose and there are no boundaries, no leverage, nothing to lean on.

It's right in the center, though, where timid and reckless are in balance, where we alternate between controlled and silly, right there... that's where we are able to make our magic.

We've each found a million places to hide. These are four of them.

Shame and failure

Failure's not fun. But failure is required. Failure in the service of learning, of experimenting, of making things—this is essential.

When you're learning to walk, no one criticizes you when you fall down. Parents understand that you do it wrong and then you do it right.

But that's about the last time you get that benefit. After that, we shame you when you fail.

We shame you as a way of gaining compliance and obedience. We shame you for your D-, we shame you for the missed shot on goal, we shame you what you wore to the dance.

Is it any wonder we associate failure with shame?

Here is the microphone

When they write the history of this revolution, the one that started twenty years ago and continues to gain steam, they might mention the rise of online retail, and it's possible that the Nest thermostat will get a mention. But clearly, the most important thing that has happened is that you've been given a microphone.

What are the most essential uses of the Internet? Email, chat, online video. Meetup, Twitter, and Facebook. eBay, Wikipedia, and Kickstarter. And they are all the same.

Every one of them is destroying the bottleneck of selection by the powerful and is instead opening the door for individuals (and organizations) to speak up, to produce work they share, and to be generous.

Thirty years ago, there were just a few business magazines. There were a few bookstores in each town, with a few hundred feet of shelf space for each section. There were three TV networks, with cable promising a few dozen more. There was CB radio, but no useful way to connect groups of people who shared similar interests. There were bullhorns, devices for yelling, but they were owned by just a few organizations.

It's entirely possible to still do your work in privacy and silence. You can be a freelance woodworker, or a bookkeeper with a few clients, or a member of the tech crew at a Broadway show.

For the rest of us, the invention of the microphone, the cheap, powerful, and ubiquitous microphone, changes everything, forever.

When did you lose your voice?

All these microphones, all this amplification, and we're stuck, unable to use them. Not because the amplifier doesn't work, but because we are unwilling to use it.

The Internet has given anyone with something to say the freedom to say it. It has given us the freedom to connect, the freedom to be generous, and the freedom to make a difference. And we (all of us) refuse to use this freedom to the fullest, because we can't bear to live with the internal narrative it would create—the narrative of responsibility and risk and failure.

To be really clear here, I don't think you've lost your voice, not at all. I think your voice is there, it always has been, but the thought that you might be able to use it is paralyzing.

Don't fight this feeling of dread. Don't fight this fear. Acknowledge it and speak, regardless.

Is it easy? Of course not. If it were easy, you'd already be doing it. Just as the marathon runner is exhausted, the person with a loud and clear voice is afraid.

But she speaks, regardless.

First in a whisper if you must, but begin.

In Nike's famous slogan, what does the word "just" mean? I overuse that word all the time in my writing—once I'm done with a book, I have to use search-and-replace to find the 178 times I wrote "just" and delete most of them.

When Nike says just do it, do they mean, "what the hell, it doesn't matter, just go ahead and do it"?

DO IT

I don't think so. As David Reynolds has written, they mean, "only do it." Do it without having an entire debate about it. Do it without creating a series of distractions about it. Do it without bargaining with the fear. *Only do it*. Do it well, better than anyone expects. Do it without apology and do it now. Only.

We rarely do something with "only." When we do, our power astonishes even us.

Why not be Spurlock?

Morgan Spurlock, of the handlebar mustache and the thirty days of eating at McDonald's, is a documentary filmmaker for our time. On a shoestring budget, he's made a series of movies and TV shows that have changed the way millions of people look at food, at the working class, and at other issues that so many of us wrestle with.

Here's a fascinating question: Why Morgan? With cameras as cheap as they are, and mustaches as easy to grow, why is there only one Morgan?

This is a hard road, the journey of the independent documentary filmmaker. But there are plenty of hard roads. Hard roads sitting in an office being an actuary. Hard roads doing repetitive labor. The daily grind of making a living in a world that doesn't seem to care as much as it should.

Those jobs, though, tend to be about being picked, about being given a slot, about having not only boundaries but also the excuse that comes from saying, "it's my job." Morgan, and those like him, don't get those excuses.

They get to live with the knowledge that it was their turn, and they took it.

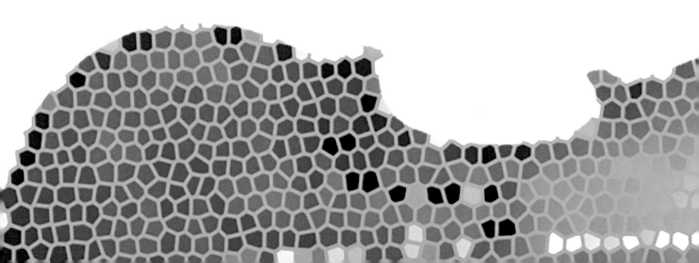

Who sold you on playing second violin?

Maestro Ben Zander has strong feelings about the appropriate mindset of the second violinist. Some people think of this role as a failure, as a stepping stone, as something to be a bit ashamed of. "Second fiddle" isn't a compliment.

In a quartet, of course, the second violin is as responsible for as much of the musical experience as the first violinist. It might be better to call the roles *this* violin and *that* violin instead of first and second.

The hierarchy inherent in so many industrial settings, though, sells us on the idea that the second violin is somehow inferior, waiting around for a chance to get picked and to be the first violin one day.

And so, no one sets out to become a second violinist, no teacher specializes in giving second-violin lessons, no one idolizes and celebrates the second violinist.

If you give up the opportunity to make your music and grudgingly settle for merely playing the music as written, you're not playing second violin, not really. You're surrendering.

The successful second violinist doesn't wait for his turn to be the first violinist. He takes advantage of the right-now, the moment he can take his turn to be the second violinist who brings it all together, who makes the music sing, who leaps.

Someone's been here before you

Memo to that newly matriculated freshman on his way to school: I know you feel quite edgy and radical wearing a tank top today, but it's been done before. In fact, every year for the last decade, a newly matriculated freshman has bravely walked in as if no one had ever done it before.

And memo to that entrepreneur who is certain that the world is about to end, because the unique set of pressures, promises and opportunities bearing down is such a perfect problem it's never been experienced quite like this before: it has.

Mostly, a memo to the struggling human who faces the abyss of taking a turn and is sure that this is the end of everything: it's not.

Promise.

Someone has been here before you.

In fact, almost everyone you admire has.

It seems like an abyss, like the valley of no return, but in fact, this is precisely the way it's supposed to feel. It's that valley that insulates this territory from the rest of our ordinary lives, that keeps this work scarce, that gives us a sense that we're doing something truly important.

Don't deny the feeling, or run from it or try to stamp it out.

Celebrate this fear and this thrill, because it's the dance you're about to do that will make the work worth doing.

WE HAVE ENDLESS CONFIDENCE IN YOU, REGARDLESS OF WHAT HAPPENED YESTERDAY AND THE DAY BEFORE THAT. THAT'S WHAT ENDLESS MEANS. YOU'LL GET THERE. MAYBE TODAY.

You'll ache. And you're going to love it. It will crush you. And you're still going to love all of it. Doesn't it sound lovely beyond belief?

Ernest Hemingway

The inevitable encroachment of mediocrity and the appeal of compromise

I made an omelet for my friend Joanne the other day. This is sort of a big deal, because she used to be the most important restaurant critic in Canada, and she has an aversion to egg-white omelets. She assured me that I had no chance whatsoever of cooking her an egg-white omelet that she'd enjoy.

Over the years, I have developed a relentless approach to an egg-white omelet, made in a cast-iron skillet with fresh herbs. Sometimes I add some peppers from the farmer's market or some spinach. It takes me less than six minutes, start to finish, including cleanup, to make breakfast.

Much to her surprise, she was delighted. The reason she'd never had a good one was that places that serve omelets for breakfast have almost universally compromised their way to mediocrity. Some questions they might ask:

Can we use a standard restaurant skillet? The cast iron is too hard to clean.

Of course you can. If you do, you'll end up with eggs that have no real color and are a little flaccid, but it'll work.

Can we use a portable propane burner instead of a real stove? It's easier for us.

Of course you can. If you do, though, you won't have a lot of heat and it'll take a long time and not taste as good.

Do we have to use fresh herbs? That'll add more than $3 a day to our costs.

Of course you don't have to use fresh herbs. The eggs won't taste as good, naturally.

I notice your omelet is sort of big; our policy is to use only three eggs, so if you want an egg-white omelet, it's going to be pretty tiny. It's not fair to give you more eggs, because it's the same price as the regular omelet. Is that okay?

Well, since eggs cost you 8 cents each, I can understand your desire to standardize and keep your costs really low. So, sure, go ahead.

You used fresh veggies as a garnish. Even though you ordered a healthy protein, we're going to give you hash browns as a garnish, because that's what everyone gets. Okay?

Sure, whatever.

You mentioned the farmer's market. We get a delivery every day from Sisco, and if it's not on the truck, we can't serve it; it takes too much time to go to a farmer's market. You understand, right?

Yep. Up to you.

Once you start compromising, when do you stop?

If your goal is to be remarkable, please understand that the easiest way to do that is to compromise less, not more. Mediocrity feels safe and easy until it's neither.

Program or be programmed

I know the words to the theme of *The Dick Van Dyke Show*. I also know that the music was written by the same guy who wrote the theme to *Perry Mason*. I have seen every episode of *The Prisoner* and just about all of *Seinfeld* as well. Which is why I'm particularly qualified to talk about not watching television or, more specifically, making the choice to be a programmer, instead of being the programmed (see Doug Rushkoff talk about this: bit.ly/programor).

Television demands passivity. It entrains us with the masses, all mesmerized by a glowing electronic hearth, all in sync, all in the service of what the media company wants to sell us.

Teams of people are working hard to get you hooked and keep you hooked, so they can profit. Twenty or more hours not spent reading, not teaching, not connecting, not experimenting, not failing, not growing, and generally not making a ruckus. For many people, it's more than fifty hours a week of not making a difference.

It's a trap that allows us to exchange our time for a place to hide out from the challenge of learning to program.

Program a computer. Program a conference. Program a blog or a book or a movie you contribute to. Make it, don't watch it.

EITHER YOU'RE THE CREATOR OR YOU'RE THE AUDIENCE. EITHER YOU'RE WAITING YOUR TURN OR YOU'RE TAKING IT.

On the hook

Some people hate this.

If it's actually up to you, if your turn is just waiting to be taken, if the microphone is right here—then who's responsible when you back away?

If acquired traits like resilience and persistence and generosity are more important than genes and talent, then who can we possibly point to when things don't go well?

It's the other people, it's the bureaucracy, it's the unfair system. Blaming anyone but us is soothing and comforting.

The alternative is to be on the hook, to see the opportunity that comes with freedom, the choice to make a difference and to matter.

Being on the hook is a privilege. It means the people around us are trusting us to contribute, counting on us to deliver.

It's not something to be avoided.

Charles Pollock was a painter

His brother Jackson, was an artist.

The reason that you've never heard of Charles is simple: He painted just like his teacher, Thomas Hart Benton did.

Benton's murals and heroic imagery represented an important turning point in American figurative art. And Jackson Pollock blew most of it up when he created action painting.

Brother Charles, though, didn't cause change, didn't take his turn, didn't choose to be on a vanguard.

Instead, he painted the way he had been taught to paint.

By a master, certainly, but still a copy.

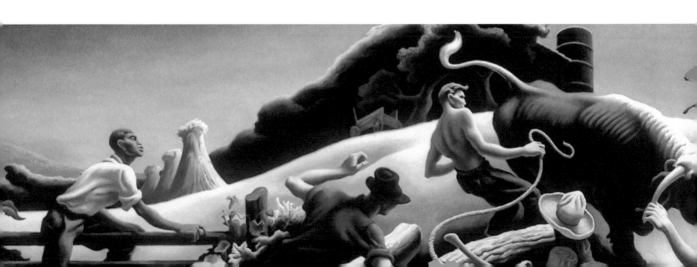

To be an artist

Is to be on the hook

To take your turn

To do things that might not work

To seek connection

To embrace generosity first

To take responsibility

To change someone

To be human

Knowledge or beauty?

John Keats, even at 24, understood what Coleridge missed. Knowledge can only fit within what we already know, within the boxes we build for it. Beauty, on the other hand, can transcend those limits.

"Negative Capability, that is when man is capable of being in uncertainties. Mysteries, doubts, without any irritable reaching after fact and reason." Doubt comes from being of two minds, yes and not-yes.

YOU DON'T DO IMPROV ONCE YOU FIGURE OUT WHAT TO SAY. YOU DO IMPROV AND THEN YOU ARE ABLE TO SAY SOMETHING.

Scratching itches

It's easy to confuse "itch" with "scratch".

They are not the same thing. You can't do anything about an itch. An itch is not an action. An itch is merely there. *Scratching is something you do.*

We have to decide when the itch of fear shows up, when the itch of the resistance shows up, when the itch of, "I better not do that" shows up, what do we do? Do we indulge the screaming lizard brain and scratch at our itch of fear?

The problem with scratching is it makes the itch worse. It engages with it.

When we bargain with the fear, we make the fear stronger.

When we rationalize the fear, we make the fear stronger.

We we seek to minimize the fear, we make the fear stronger.

The only thing we can do about itches is celebrate them and dance with them. We gain the upper hand, seeing the itch as fear and using it as a compass, "Ah I remember the last time I thought I shouldn't do something and it worked out. This is another one of those. I'm going to go do that thing, not scratch the itch."

Suddenly, we're using it to help us, to point us toward where we want to go.

What artists do, again and again, is look for the itches, and instead of scratching them— we embrace the itch instead.

Did DaVinci go to the Maker Faire?

What about Rembrandt? It's hard to imagine the two of them meeting at a conference to discuss whether or not it was okay for them to go ahead and create (as opposed to merely consume).

When I was growing up, like a lot of kids, I had a chemistry kit. I also had an eletronics kit, but they were very different.

My electronics kit said on the cover "101 ways to build with electronics." The deluxe kit had 191 ways. Clearly, volume counted.

You would put these little electronic blocks together step by step, hook up a battery and you would have a working radio. If you put them together differently, you could also make a radio. There was a third way to make a radio. Pretty much, all of these things were about making a radio or possibly a doorbell.

This was totally different than the chemistry kit. It was one of those *real* chemistry kits with actual dangerous chemicals in it, not the more modern safe kind. Sulfurous smoke would come belching out of our basement, some things would explode, other things would start on fire—the chemistry kit was all about failing. The chemistry kit was about coming up with hundreds of ways to mix things together that wouldn't work precisely as planned, whereas the electronic kit was about following step by step by step through a little grid they gave you to demonstrate how to make a radio.

Kits! Kits are the training ground for factory workers of tomorrow. Lego kits, jigsaw puzzles—they're fun, they have a place, but they're not about making anything. Making is failing until you figure out what works. Making is dancing with success and failure at the same time. Making is leaping.

DaVinci didn't do kits.

"You snotty-faced heap of parrot droppings"

Michael Palin and John Cleese did the greatest Monty Python sketch of all time, and it involves going to an argument clinic.

Michael Palin walks in, he pays his one quid, and he says, "I'd like to have an argument, please."

The receptionist says, "Ahh yes, Try Mr. Barnard; room 12."

Palin opens the door of room 12. One of the other Pythons is there, and the guy starts abusing him.

He's totally taken aback, then he realizes he's opened the wrong door. This isn't the argument room. This is the abuse room. So he shuts that door, he walks down the door to the next room, and there's Cleese. Cleese does a poor job of arguing. They have an argument about arguing, and it's going on with a lot of spirit.

Then, suddenly, Cleese stops. Palin says, "What?"

Cleese responds, "Sorry, the five minutes is up."

The question is, why are we living this sketch daily? Why do we go to actual rooms where actual people make us feel badly? Why do we seek out endless feedback online from people (often anonymous) who dislike or distrust us? Why expose ourselves to all these itches, merely so we can scratch them?

With the same amount of effort, you can walk into the "egg me on" room. Or the room filled with enthusiasm. Or the room with problems ready to be solved.

THESE ARE STATES OF MIND, AVAILABLE TO US WHENEVER WE CHOOSE THEM.

Give credit

Organizations are built on credit, and sometimes it seems as though personal careers are too. Not just who is responsible for good work, but the inverse: *whom can I blame?*

When the sky is cloudless and blue and people are itching to do something that matters, the single easiest way to get something to move forward is to relentlessly give away credit for what you created.

Don't fret: This is not your only victory; this is not the only time you'll have something important to say or generous to contribute. Give it away.

And soon, people will want to work with you again. Because they know that you'll give them credit.

Soon, there will be a line of people out your door, eager to get credit for your best work.

Which means that you'll begin to get meta-credit as the person to go to for ideas that other people can take credit for. Which is just fine.

Take blame

The other side of giving credit is taking blame.

Why on earth would you want to take blame for something that's not your fault? Or, now and then, for something that is?

Because taking blame takes guts. Because it's something that grownups can handle. Because it's not fatal.

And most of all, because the person who is responsible enough to be responsible discovers that it's her turn more often.

Don't listen

Your customers and teachers and peers don't actually know what they want. If they did, they'd build it or buy it instead of waiting for you to show up and take your turn.

Steve Jobs didn't listen to customers asking for the iPod and the iPhone. There weren't any.

Henry Ford didn't listen to people

asking for a car that cost a third of what other cars did. There weren't any.

When we listen, we're giving ourselves a safety net, doing work that's easy to excuse, because, of course, it was someone else's idea.

We need your idea, please.

Perfectionism

Suppose you were challenged to turn the Earth into a perfect sphere. *When would we be done?*

Fill in the Grand Canyon, level Mt. Everest, it's a never-ending challenge to make the Earth perfectly smooth. It's easy to understand a certain kind of perfectionism, one that would claim that the Earth is never ready to be announced as smooth.

Here's the thing: if we shrunk the Earth, the Earth we live on right now, to the size of a basketball, it would be the smoothest sphere of its kind ever created. The Grand Canyon wouldn't be noticed by anything short of an electron microscope at this scale. Sure, the perfectionists could correctly state that the Earth could be even more perfectly round, but surely the roundest thing ever seen is round enough.

Steal ideas

We seek out the safe harbor of being completely original as another place to hide, because it's impossible to be original. So, when we see a competitor or someone who has done something remotely like our work, we stop. Too late, this one is taken.

There are countless varieties of original, productive work, and all of them are based on something that has been done before. Your recombination, your generous reshuffling of what we already have, is the first step on the way to producing work that matters to us. Steal, give credit and ship...

Ship

UNTIL YOUR WORK INTERACTS WITH THE MARKET, IT'S AS IF THERE IS NO WORK.

The market is many things—the boss who has seen your report, the donor who has heard your pitch, the investor who has reviewed your business plan. Until you put that work in front of someone you are trying to change, though, it doesn't exist.

When we ship our work, we cross a chasm. It goes from <here>, where it's safe, untouched by the world, perfect in our heads, to <there>, where it is beaten up, misunderstood, and most of all, a slate where others can write down their dreams and fears.

Change things quietly and avoid the no-people

One of the safest (and of course, most tempting) ways to make change happen in an organization is to get buy-in early and often. To go to the boss, to lay out the plan, to make your case, and to get her to say yes. Or even better, to say, "YES!"

We'd like carte blanche. When King Charles the Second was fleeing the Roundheads, he offered his men signed sheets of paper*, blank at the top, giving them complete deniability via his signature. What could be better? Power without responsibility. Authority to make change happen. Complete bureaucratic safety.

This never works.

It never works because your boss is all out of white paper. Because people don't keep their jobs in organizations by saying yes to big, untested initiatives. Because if someone is going to say yes, they're not going to say it to you.

Building bridges not burning them

Every interaction, every moment when it's your turn, is an opportunity. It's also a choice about whether to build or to take.

When we connect with someone else, are we enhancing our relationship with him or taking something instead? When we talk to a customer service rep, or to a spiritual leader or a stranger on the street, are we building something or tearing it down?

In the polished, industrialized, zipless modern world, some people would like every interaction to be similar to the way we deal with an ATM. You don't say "thank you." You don't say "please." You push the buttons and money comes out.

As humans, though, we can do better than this; we can actually leave something better than we found it. A non-digital, non-corporate transaction deserves to be human, real, and personal.

Teaching others scales right back to us

If I give you this bag of beans, I won't have any more beans. Beans are scarce.

If I teach you how to throw a Frisbee, I'll still know how to throw one. And you will, too. The game is infinite if we choose it be.

Once more of us know how, we'll be able to play together.

Teaching rewards us all.

Could it be love?

One reason to write a book is to work out ideas.

As I began to wrap up this one, I came to a realization: The art I'm talking about, the bravery, the generosity... it's just another way of talking about love.

When we fall in love, there are no guarantees. No promise that it will be reciprocated or last forever, or even meet our imagined needs.

The act of loving a person, an idea, a quest—it's the same duality as the experience of taking your turn. Knowing that it might not work. Embracing the fact that it might. Doing it more for others than for yourself.

And when it doesn't work, doing it again.

• • •

The leap into this space is a form of love.

To love in the purest sense of the word, not the love of loving a candy bar or some other need, fulfilled. The love of being generous at great expense, of sticking with something that doesn't work right away, of not only surviving the fear of rejection but embracing it.

And the joy of being supported and believed in and embraced by people you care about, even when it's not working, even when it's a total disaster.

I guess this is why I'm so evangelical about our ability to choose ourselves, and why I'm so mystified by those who willingly give up the privilege in exchange for something that feels like safety.

I can't imagine how empty it would be to choose a life focused on selfish needs and the lack of love that this entails. A life built around merely making a profit, or avoiding things that might go wrong, and making sure to be off the hook at every turn.

What a chance we have then, to bring love to our work life, to our creative lives, to the community we choose to embrace. What an opportunity to experience, as viscerally as we dare, the feeling of this might not work, of ever closer connections to people that mean something to us and most of all, of making a difference, of choosing to matter.

We shouldn't deny these feelings, any more than we should deny the magic of loving (and being loved by) another human being. The complexity and juiciness of it all is precisely the point, isn't it?

At the end of giving a speech, or teaching a class or writing a book, I feel a pang of sadness. For a few minutes or hours or months, I've created a new reality, drawn a castle in the clouds, one that I hope has resonated.

And then it's gone, the act of creating is over, all the remains is the change I've been able to make in other people.

All so I can do it again.

So *we* can do it again.

Go, make your ruckus.

With love.

Acknowledgments

Joanne Kates, Rohan Rajiv, Carla Lisio, Abraham Joshua Heschel, Ben & Roz Zander, Jodi Sagorin, David Reynolds, Winnie Kao, Alan Kuras, Catherine E. Oliver, Steven Dennis, Doug Rushkoff, Daniel Heller-Roazen, Steve Pressfield, Lisa DiMona, Andrew Kendall, Julie Burstein, Shawn Coyne, Hugh Macleod, Sharon Rowe, Teri Tobias, Isaac Asimov, Cory Doctorow, Mark Frauenfelder, Fred Wilson, Sasha Dichter, Ishita Gupta, Jacqueline Novogratz, Bernadette Jiwa, Bob McKinnon, Brian Koppelman, Tami Simon, Dominique Gibert, Niki Papadapolous, Adrian Zackheim, Kevin Kelly, Steve Pressfield, Tom Peters, Jo-Ann Tan, Mitch Joel, Clay Hebert, Jonathan Sackner Bernstein and Kerissa Catania.

Photo processing: Polo Jimenez
Design coach: Alex Miles Younger

thanks, Dad

Every one of you made a difference in my life and to this book. Thank you.

Dedicated to Marjorie.

And to Mo, who instigated this one, Alex who cheered, and Helene for always.

Photo credits

Unless otherwise stated, all photos are public domain, Creative Commons licensed or considered fair use.

Cover photo by Noel Besuzzi (boshimages.com). Escalator video shots courtesy of Tim Piper. Defintely check out the video. Agenda session photo by Seth Godin. Humpty is a hand-recolored public domain image. Mek tribesman used with permission of Corbis. Victorian dress remixed by Olex Oleole at oleole.tumblr.com. Carole Gieseke lent us her roller coaster image. Dunes shot by Luca Galuzzi. Sundial by Michael Glasgow. Swimming baby by Phil Shaw Photography at londonbabyswim.co.uk. Woodpile by Ken Woodhead at Kenwoodart.com. Monk's notes captured by Steve Lacy. Neil Gaiman courtesy of Kyle Cassidy. Pictures in Kenya by me. Photo of canoeing instruction by Leon Muszynski. Janis Joplin, like many of the images here, from Wikimedia Commons. Neil Young thanks to Phil King/Man Alive. Microphone courtesy of Tome Wilson. Fried egg shot by me, on cast iron. Thomas Hart Benton WPA murals from the Smithsonian. Lizard licensed via istock. Skull and Crossbones by Ryan Lerch. Hugh MacLeod cartoon courtesy of Gaping Void. The blue photo on the last spread is the sky in the south of France, via Wikimedia Commons. Article on the very last page from *Good Housekeeping*.

Many images tweaked by me and by Polo Jimenez (www.polojimenez.com). Thanks Polo.

Printed in Canada by Hemlock. Ask for Kerissa and tell her I sent you.

Written and designed by Seth Godin. Find more at sethgodin.com

To inquire about bulk purchases and international rights, please visit yourturn.link

PRINTED IN CANADA

Ruth Ann Harnisch, Mary Whitcomb, John Jantsch, M Walsh, Mike Lloyd, Jeff Kurpuis

Find the

*Books don't change people. People change people.

We do it by sharing ideas, by setting standards, by making it clear that people like us do things like this. As Timothy Leary said, once you figure things out, your job is to find the others. Together, we will change things.

Please share this copy with your team and with people you care about. You can get more by visiting: www.yourturn.link

others*

Who should read this next? Write your name and then pass on this copy...

_____ _____

_____ _____

_____ _____

_____ _____

_____ _____

_____ _____

_____ _____

> "WE ARE THE ONES WE
> HAVE BEEN WAITING FOR"
>
> INSPIRED BY FARID UD-DIN ATTAR

From an account by Emmeline Pankhurst, mother of Christine, who was Annie Kennie's cellmate and co-leader in the fight for the right to vote. Christine was inspired by her meeting with Susan B. Anthony. But it all came down to Annie and Christine taking their turn. From *Good Housekeeping* Magazine.

The First Prison Sentence

Of course the affair created a tremendous sensation, not only in Manchester, where my husband had been so well known and where I had so long held public office, but all over England. The comments of the press were almost unanimously bitter. Ignoring the perfectly well-established fact that men in every political meeting ask questions and demand answers of the speakers, the newspapers treated the action of the two girls as something quite unprecedented and outrageous. They generally agreed that great leniency had been shown them. Fines and jail sentences were too good for such unsexed creatures. "The discipline of the nursery" would have been far more appropriate. One Birmingham paper declared that "if any argument were required against giving ladies political status and power, it has been furnished in Manchester." Newspapers which had heretofore ignored the whole subject now hinted that while they had formerly been in favor of women's suffrage, they could no longer countenance it. The Manchester incident, it was said, had set the cause back, perhaps irrevocably.

Those women had followed me to the House of Commons. They had defied the police. They were awake at last. They were prepared to do something that women had never done before—fight for themselves. Women have always fought for men, and for their children. Now they were ready to fight for their own human rights. Our militant movement was established.